FAITH FOR A
LIFETIME

FAITH FOR A LIFETIME

A Spiritual Journey

Archbishop Iakovos

**PRIMATE OF THE GREEK ORTHODOX ARCHDIOCESE
OF NORTH AND SOUTH AMERICA**

with William Proctor

Doubleday

NEW YORK
1988

Library of Congress Cataloging-in-Publication Data
Iakovos, Archbishop of the Greek Orthodox Archdiocese of North and
South America.
   Faith for a lifetime: a spiritual journey/Archbishop Iakovos with Wil-
liam Proctor—1st ed.
      p.   cm.
   ISBN 0-385-19595-8
   1. Spiritual life—Orthodox Eastern authors.   2. Iakovos,
Archbishop of the Greek Orthodox Archdiocese of North and South Amer-
ica.   I. Proctor, William.   II. Title.
BX382.I34   1988
248.4'819—dc19   87-24158
                                                                CIP

Contents

PART III   THE PUBLIC WAY

FAITH FOR A
LIFETIME

PART I

WHAT IS
THE INNER WAY?

PART I

WHAT IS
THE INNER WAY?

The Way of the Child

A few years ago, in a large American city, I was engaging in small talk with some families who had gathered in a sitting room. During a lull in the conversation, a three-year-old walked up to me rather boldly and asked, "Can you come with me?"

"Yes," I replied. I was rather impressed that this little boy would be brave enough to take the initiative with a strange grown-up—especially one whose face was covered with white beard and who was dressed in the long black robes and imposing neck cross of the Orthodox clergy.

But this youngster was completely undaunted. He took my hand and led me to a corner of the room, away from the other guests. Almost before I could bend down to his level, he put his important question to me: "How can I see God?"

That's a hard question coming from anyone. But it's particularly difficult when you're dealing with a three-year-old.

On a superficial level, whenever I encounter such a question from a young child—and I've heard it in a number times during my lifetime—I find myself fishing for the response which is true, yet which will also satisfy an inquisitive but still undeveloped young mind. How do you pick just the right words to provide food now for spiritual infancy, and perhaps also nudge the youngster toward a more developed faith in the future?

In this case, I referred to the Scriptures for my answer: "Jesus said that those who are pure or clean in heart will be happy because they will see God. If your heart stays clean, as I know it is now, you'll certainly see God. But remember, most often we don't see God on the outside with our eyes. Instead, we see him on the inside, with our hearts."

Of course, the full implications of such an answer will sink in only gradually, over many years of study, prayer and worship. But the important thing is to keep the words of Christ circulating among us, to scatter them here and there, like seeds from the sower until they find fertile ground in a receptive heart.

Such questions from children are disturbing for me, not just because it's hard to find just the right response for a young spirit, but also because the question enters my own heart and becomes my personal prayer for understanding. Immediately after I heard this boy ask me how he could see God, I found myself asking silently, "How can *I* see God?"

I always look deep inside myself at such times to see if I have the clean and pure heart that Jesus said in his Beatitudes I must have if I am to see the Father. Often, if I feel unprepared to answer the youngster's question, I know that it's not really the child asking me for an answer: It's God. He has a way of conveying his special messages to us through the words of other people, including children.

I'm particularly thankful when God conveys a message to me through a child because that experience always reminds me that the lifelong, inner journey with Christ on this earth begins with a childlike faith and attitude. As Jesus himself said, "Truly I say to you, unless you turn and become like children you will never enter the kingdom of heaven." (Matthew 18:3, RSV)

Why is the way of the child so basic for the Christian's inner journey? Jesus pointed us toward the answer in that same passage from the Gospel of Matthew: "Whoever humbles himself like this child, he is the greatest in the kingdom of heaven." (Matthew 18:4, RSV)

And how does a child humble himself? He doesn't trust in his own mental or physical powers. Rather, he just accepts everything as his parents offer it. In every case when a child comes to me and I give him something, he accepts without any questions. He trusts. He assumes that I love him.

It's the same way when we, as children of God, relate to our Heavenly Father. We have to trust him and accept what he offers us as true and valid. When Jesus tells you that the Kingdom of God is within you, you don't have to go around "shopping" here and there to try to find it. Rather, he means for you just to take his words at face value—much as a child would accept what's offered by his parents.

So the inner way of the Christian life—the way that leads to spiritual growth and progress—is the child's way. This doesn't mean being childish, of course, but rather childlike. The child*ish* traveler on this spiritual road may whine, become distracted, display a short attention span and be overcome by impatience when things don't happen as quickly as he wants or in quite the way he expects. The child*like* traveler, in contrast, will wait on the Lord. He'll always believe that God loves him and never doubt that the appropriate fruits of faith will come in their own good time.

Above all, the way of the child, which Jesus has urged us to follow, involves establishing and cultivating a relationship. Just as the human child grows and blossoms to his full potential in the care of loving parents, so, as human beings pursue their spiritual journey, they must walk in the care and nurturance of a loving Divine Parent. But how do we pursue this relationship with the Heavenly Father? What are the specific means and disciplines that enable us to cultivate and strengthen our relationship with our Heavenly Parent?

In the following pages, I'll share with you in some detail my own personal observations and experiences on the inner way of the Christian life. First, we'll consider some of the private roads of spiritual development, including personal prayer and meditation; the meaning of faith; the place of adoration and worship during the spiritual journey; and the Bible as the bedrock of faith. Also, we'll contemplate the centrality of the cross; the way memories play a key role in spiritual growth; the meaning of time, life, and love; and God's peace as an antidote for anxiety, burnout, and fear.

But these primarily private disciplines and concerns reflect only one side of our developing relationship with Christ. Simultaneously, we must also look to the more public highways and byways of spiritual growth. What I have in mind here are such things as these: Seeking true unity with other believers through God's Spirit . . . Experiencing the joy, nurturance, and correction of Christian community—or the power of *koinonia*, to use the New Testament Greek . . . Understanding how to conduct an authentic, life-changing dialogue with others . . . Seeing that servanthood is the end, not simply the means of spiritual development . . . Developing a spirit-infused marriage relationship and . . . Truly *living* the mystical, exhilarating liturgy of the church.

Of course, even as I mention some of these paths of spiritual growth, I certainly don't want to suggest that I think I've "arrived" at any semblance of the ultimate goal of spiritual perfection. Even St. Paul, who had advanced to a stage of inner growth that I can never hope to attain, admitted openly that he had fallen short. He wrote to the church at Philippi: "Not that I have already obtained this or am already perfect; but I press on to make it my own, because Christ Jesus has made me his own." (Philippians 3:12, RSV)

But still, even though you and I know we are not perfect and will never become perfect on this earth, we must press on toward the goal that Christ has set for us. As little children, we must pursue the inner way of spiritual development and trust, in the sure knowledge that our Parent will indeed live up to his promises—and guide us, imperfect as we are, into his realm of perfection. The way of the child, in a very special way, *is* the way of perfection. But as we'll see next, this way takes time, patience and staying power for those who hope to find the ultimate prize near their grasp.

2

The Way to Perfection

God wants you to be perfect.

Jesus could hardly have made this point more clearly than when he proclaimed in his Sermon on the Mount, "Therefore you are to be perfect, as your heavenly Father is perfect." (Matthew 5:48, NASB)

But how can we, rebellious, deficient, and mistake-prone creatures that we are, achieve this perfection? On its face, this demand seems unreasonable because it's impossible. Yet the impossible is the point where Jesus began when he commented on how difficult it is for a rich man to enter the Kingdom of Heaven. Christ said, "With men this is impossible, but with God all things are possible." (Matthew 19:26, NASB)

The way of perfection, then, is certainly beyond the power of any human being; but it's *not* beyond the power of God. Still, how can a mere mortal embark on this path toward perfection? Even more important, can a human being hope to approach or achieve perfection in this life? And what does it mean to become perfect as God is perfect?

These are difficult questions—perhaps the most difficult that you or I will ever face. Moreover, they're not abstract, intellectual queries that could satisfy us in a pleasant theological debate over dinner one evening. Rather, these questions are profoundly disturbing. Also, they carry highly practical implications because they go to the very heart of what life on this earth is all about.

In the New Testament, the Greek word for "perfect" is *teleios,* though the term is sometimes translated "mature" or "maturity." I myself prefer those meanings that imply growing, developing, or becoming perfect, rather than the idea of having already become mature. Too often, the concept of maturity may give us a sense that it's possible to "arrive" at a particular spiritual state. Yet I don't think that's possible at all! The way of perfection is just that—it's a way or path that leads us *toward* the image of the One who is perfect, Jesus Christ. But we won't "check in" to that final destination until we're with him permanently.

St. Paul talks about being guided by the Spirit, or "walking" in the Spirit of God, right to the very end of our lives. We must grow, Paul says, in the faith and knowledge of Christ. But at all times, Christ remains the ultimate standard and driving force in our lives.

He's not just a historic person who is my model, a kind of detached example toward whom I must strive. Rather, as the Scriptures say, he is the same yesterday, today, and forever. As such, he is always inviting me and challenging me to live my whole life in a way that will eventually lead to perfection. But the way is an ongoing journey that begins in this life, but never quite ends here. Again, as St. Paul says, I am not yet perfect, but I press on to lay hold of that which Christ offers to me.

Yet even as Christ beckons to us and challenges us to press forward toward His perfection, he can do so only from within us. If I succeed in bringing him inside, then I can feel him and hear him. I can know what he wants, expects, and demands of me. Otherwise, he remains a lifeless historic icon before whom I may cross myself or offer a kiss, without experiencing true spiritual power.

Yet how does he get inside your being and become the motivation and will that propels you along the spiritual path? The answer is rather simple: You must receive him. Perhaps the most powerful image can be found in the Apocalypse, where St. John reports Jesus as saying that he is standing and knocking at your door.

Jesus often knocks on your door in those times when you have nowhere else to go. Those are the occasions when you can trust no one, when you are without friends, when you are rejected or feel unaccepted by others. At other points, you may hear his knock as you're being led or taught by some other human being you trust. These are the times to invite him in and engage in a dialogue with him.

Jesus first began to knock on my door when I was a child, and the person he used to start me on his way of perfection was one I trusted totally, my own mother.

I had an exceptional mother. Her strong, deep faith reflected golden rays of God's love, which finally found a place in my heart. My mother was a woman of prayer, though she never read prepared prayers or repeated those which had been copied in some book. Her conversation with God was just that —conversation, a natural talking, back and forth, as one person would talk to another.

I received all my early religious education from my mother, and she taught me in such a way that her instruction continues to occupy an important place in my mind and heart. Even when I spoke with my mother about God at the very tender age of three or four, she never tried to impose her wish or will on me. She never discussed or tried to influence my future or my faith, at least not in pushy, didactic terms. Instead, she just prayed that the will of God be done in my life.

What did she really want for me?

Although she never told me so, I'm fairly sure she didn't want me to become a priest. Her uncle had become an abbot in a monastery, and her brother was a deacon and a student of theology. She had lost both of them to the church, and both had died young. I sometimes had the feeling that she didn't want to lose her own son. But she never told me her desires in so many words. She just continued to pray for God's will.

In fact, it was God's will, and not her human will, that was finally done in my life. Gradually, as I passed through my teens and early twenties, I was drawn more and more to God and to serving him in the church. After I had completed several years of theological education, I began to do some preaching and to work as a Sunday school teacher in the largest village on my native island, Imbros, which was under Turkish rule.

Apparently, I did rather well as a Sunday school teacher because many adults and children flocked to the church to hear my lessons. But this response from the people created some serious problems for me with the Turkish authorities. Since the time that Constantinople had been conquered by the Turks, they had refused to allow their subjects to have churches or positions of any type that were higher or more impressive than those of the Turks. So, as more people came to our church, we became more vulnerable.

Soon, my worst fears were realized. One day, as I descended from the pulpit, a Turkish policeman intercepted me and barked, "You come with me!"

So I followed him out of the church. I was immediately taken to the local police station and told in no uncertain terms not to climb into that pulpit again or to teach religion in that church anymore. The charge against me? They claimed they had information that I was teaching the Greek people to be disloyal to Turkey.

Of course, these accusations were completely false. But I was faced with a choice: What was I to do with myself, now that I couldn't work in this church any longer?

I found myself in a very difficult position, spiritually and emotionally. I wanted to follow God's will for my life, but what was it? It was very difficult for me to sort through my deepest inner thoughts and feelings and determine what it was I wanted and needed—and what God wanted for me.

Certainly, my family needed my help because we were not rich. So I felt I had an obligation to start repaying them for the money they had spent on me while I was pursuing my studies. But when I was offered a position as a teacher in a high school in Constantinople—a job that would have helped cover some of my expenses—I didn't accept it. Somehow, as I thought and prayed about it, that option just didn't seem right.

What I really wanted to do, at least from a human point of view, was to leave Turkey and study abroad, preferably at the Sorbonne in Paris. An exchange program had been set up, and I had some connections that should have made my entry into the university rather easy. But for a variety of reasons, my admission to the Sorbonne and any possibility of my departing from Turkey were delayed indefinitely.

Once again, I had to confront myself and my future directly. The inner crisis I was experiencing became even deeper and more painful for me. Finally, my former dean at my seminary, who was now the Metropolitan Bishop of Derkon, had heard about my encounter with the Turkish police. He thought it was wrong that I should be subjected to such humiliation. So he wrote to me, "I have an opening for a preacher and archdeacon in my diocese. Would you like to take this position?"

I was honored to be offered this job, and of course I began to consider the idea quite seriously. I also tried to get in touch with my main spiritual director, the Metropolitan Bishop of our island, whose name was also Iakovos. But at the time, he was unavailable, on a pilgrimage to Mount Sinai. As a result, there was no way for me to communicate with him or ask his opinion.

So I was thrown back on my own spiritual resources. As young as I was in the faith, I had to make my own decision in personal consultation with God. The only thing I could do was pray.

Soon, God answered. On November 11, 1934, I had a dramatic, moving dream. In the dream, I saw Jesus sitting in front of a desk before an open window, which looked out on the street of my village. As I walked down toward the window, I noticed Jesus there. I knew beyond any doubt who it was because he looked exactly as he does in a painting by Hoffmann, with a white tunic, blond beard, and beautiful hair tumbling down his neck.

As soon as I saw him, I retreated under a huge walnut tree along the side of the road. I don't know why I ran away, but I did. But then, I decided to come out again and face him, and I saw that he was calling. He was calling *me*, saying, "Come, follow me."

The meaning of the dream was clear to me. The next day, I told my parents that I would be returning to Constantinople, that I would be ordained as a deacon, and that I would accept the position as preacher of the diocese there. In fact, as it turned out, my father also had a dream that confirmed the path on which God had put me. He later told my mother that in his dream, I was watching over big flocks on the slopes of the large mountains where my village was located. But his dream showed him that I was going to become separate from this flock—and in fact, that's exactly what I did. My decision to leave for Constantinople was just a first step in an increasing separation from my home, though not separation from God's will.

For me, these events marked the beginning of my own journey toward perfection, toward the ultimate hope for every Christian of being one with Christ, completely conformed to his image. Many things have happened to me in the decades that have followed those early decisions and encounters with Christ. Although I'm now in my seventies, I'm still on this path, moving toward perfection—though I must acknowledge that I haven't by any means reached the ultimate goal. But I still press forward, still try to keep my eyes on Jesus, the perfecter of our faith.

In the intervening years, I've faced many crises and challenges to my faith, but they've been necessary for inner growth to take place. Faith is God's gift to human beings, but it's a gift that comes to us over time. True faith comes only after years of searching, testing, and experiencing God's love in the practical situations in life.

This trusting relationship with God doesn't come simply

by intellectual inquiry or debate, however. In fact, theologians who rely too heavily on the ability of their minds to conceive the truth about God may find themselves stepping off the path that leads to perfection, and into the quicksands of heresy and doubt. Certainly, I don't undervalue the need for a healthy, inquiring mind. But I think it's a big mistake to assume that spiritual growth or insight depends on abstract thought or scholarly dialogue.

Also, in my experience, true faith usually isn't born magically or miraculously—say, after a devastating auto accident, where a person discovers that the one who saved him was Christ. Of course, such tragedies or difficulties can serve as benchmarks or signposts on the path to perfection. But much more is involved in the development of a deep and abiding relationship with God.

In short, an authentic understanding of God and sensitivity to his will can come only through time, punctuated by a multitude of experiences, many of which involve the mundane events of life, rather than dramatic, spectacular occurrences. In my own case, I see my mother's quiet, ongoing instruction and prayers as the decisive force in preparing me to receive, understand, and obey that dream that led me away from my home to Constantinople. It was the primary influence over time, setting me on the course that has shaped the rest of my life.

The specific means and disciplines that will move you along the inner way toward the perfection of Christ are included in more detail in later chapters in this book. At this point, I just want to highlight these two important principles, which define the way to perfection on which you have embarked.

First, as Jesus said, God is our ultimate standard of

perfection. He has set the course for us, just as he has given us his Son to serve as our inner guide as we move toward the ultimate goal and prize, which involves complete union with him. For Christ to fulfill this role in our lives, however, we must answer his knock; we must invite him in; we must receive him.

Secondly, we must recognize that this way to perfection will take time; in fact, it will take our entire lives. We'll never see the full glory of God until we're finally with him, in his heavenly abode. I, as much as anyone, should understand this time factor. After all, I have been moving along this inner way for more than five decades, since my dream of Christ when I was only twenty-three years old!

But in addition to these two basic principles, there's also a third that is important to understand at the very beginning of your spiritual journey: That's the importance of having a spiritual director, a more mature believer to guide you across the rough places that you will surely encounter en route to the ultimate destination. Now, let's turn our attention to the essential role that is played by the spiritual mentor.

3

A Guide for the Journey

In some ways, the Christian faith is like a flowing river, which passes in a steady spiritual stream from parent to child to grandchild.

To be sure, faith must well up in the individual heart through independent awakening and commitment. But still, our personal faith depends heavily upon the teaching, guidance, and direction that we, as individuals, have received from fellow believers who have gone before, and also from those who constitute the contemporary, living church.

In short, the Christian faith cannot flourish in a vacuum. With a few rare exceptions, belief has never sprung forth and bloomed as a desert flower, completely apart from a sustaining garden of *koinonia,* or Christian community.

How can individual faith best be nurtured by the community? One of the most effective ways is through what I call the spiritual mentor or spiritual director. Every individual believer needs a guide, a more experienced Christian who can "show him the ropes" of the spiritual life and expedite his progress in following the inner way.

Why do we need such a guide? First of all, no neophyte who is attempting to negotiate the intricate pathways of the spiritual life can possibly hope to learn everything by individual spiritual disciplines, such as personal Bible study or prayer. The Christian faith is a *lived* experience, and, as such, it must be demonstrated and explained by those who have had some experience in the dynamic interactions of life.

Also, as we've already seen, the inner way is the way of the child, characterized by a humble, trusting, and dependent posture in relation to God and his representatives on earth. The kind of humility that Jesus said we need can only come as we count others better than ourselves, and submit ourselves to those who are more advanced in the faith than we.

Submission, humility, and dependence—these are not qualities or attributes that get high marks in the corporate world or in the achievement-oriented atmosphere where most of us function each day. Yet these very qualities, Jesus said, must become indelibly impressed upon our characters if we hope to move farther along that road to perfection, which ultimately leads to perfect union with the Son and the Father.

There are plenty of biblical precedents for learning humility, dependence, and faith through submission to a spiritual mentor or director. Consider Jesus himself. His words to his disciples were "Follow me." The strength of their faith and their potential for greatness were measured by how seriously they followed his lead in becoming the servants of others. Finally, eleven of his disciples—even the worst doubter of them all, Thomas—acknowledged him as their ultimate director by calling him "Master" and "Lord."

This mentor-apprentice bond, for which Jesus and his disciples serve as the ultimate model, continued in the early church in such relationships as the one involving Paul and Timothy. As you may recall, Paul was in Lystra on his second missionary journey when he met Timothy. Young Timothy is described in the Book of Acts as "the son of a Jewish woman who was a believer; but his father was a Greek." At this meeting, a relationship began that soon blossomed into a deep and abiding bond between a spiritual father and a spiritual son.

Paul asked Timothy to accompany him on his further travels; he circumcised the younger man to make him more acceptable to the Jews who heard the Gospel; and he invested in his young charge great spiritual responsibilities. We know from Paul's letters that Timothy's faith began with the influence of his grandmother Lois and his mother Eunice. But Paul helped bring power to that faith through the laying on of hands and the bestowal of spiritual gifts. Paul urged Timothy to exercise his gifts with a "spirit of power and love and self-control."

Also, Paul addressed Timothy in his letters as "my true child of the faith" and "my beloved child." Clearly, we have here a relationship in which a spiritual father was acting as a guide and mentor for a spiritual son. And what an explosive impact these two had on the growth of the early church!

I identify strongly with Timothy because I've experienced a relationship with a spiritual father, much like the tie he must have enjoyed with St. Paul. Who was my spiritual mentor? Actually, three or four people have had a major impact on my spiritual development. As I mentioned, one of the most important people in shaping my faith was my own mother. But as I moved through my teenage years and into adulthood, another figure assumed overriding importance: Archbishop Iakovos of Derkon.

I first met this great man in 1927 when I was about eighteen years old. He was a trustee of the theological school which I attended in Constantinople, and I was quite fortunate that he took me under his wing early in my academic career. Although my spiritual father was a great mystic, he was by no means an ivory-tower type. He was jailed twice by the political authorities for his independent thinking. They burned his books because many of them were thought to be too anti-Islamic. These persecutions and other challenges he faced during his life gave him a strong moral stature, to which I was exposed and from which I benefited at an early age.

At first, my mentor behaved somewhat distantly toward me. I suppose he was trying to see if I was really serious about the spiritual journey that I had begun. But even though I lacked the wisdom and understanding that come with age, he was drawn to me as his spiritual child. He told my father, "You don't have to worry about his needs. I will take care of him."

During the first couple of years that Iakovos of Derkon advised me at school, he suggested that I not go home to my island of Imbros during the summer months. Rather, he said, I should stay near him at the school. I suppose he wanted to see whether I was independent, sensitive, and responsible enough to be worthy of a position of responsibility in the church. In any case, he watched me closely to see whether, as an honor student, I inflated myself over others. He knew that I had come from humble beginnings at Imbros, and he apparently wanted to be sure that I could retain some of that humility in the more sophisticated environment of the city.

Of course, I didn't always live up to his expectations.

Sometimes, I became quite proud of my accomplishments, and I didn't hesitate to let others know how good I was. But when he noticed even a hint of arrogance creeping into my behavior, he would say, "You'll stop acting this way, not because I say so, but because you know you should always be mindful of the gifts you've received from God."

That was all it took. Thoroughly chastened, I would go "back to the drawing boards" of my spiritual life and try to plot out a more productive course of action.

Over the years, Archbishop Iakovos of Derkon became many things for me: my teacher, my guide, my spiritual father, my companion with whom I shared my greatest dreams, my strict disciplinarian, and my spiritual tester. He always probed and checked to see whether I was truly following that inner way toward perfection that Jesus had shown us so long ago.

You might ask, "How did you know this man was the right spiritual director for you? Also, what standards should control the selection of such a director?"

Those are good questions because the spiritual realm is quite powerful and easily abused. When a strong spiritual bond is established between two people, forces may be unleashed which can be dangerous, especially if the director or mentor is not reliable and trustworthy.

Paul warns young Timothy against this sort of person when he says that "the time is coming when people will not endure sound teaching, but having itching ears they will accumulate for themselves teachers to suit their own likings, and will turn away from listening to the truth and wander into myths. As for you, always be steady, endure suffering, do the work of an evangelist, fulfill your ministry." (2 Timothy 4:3–5, RSV)

But in my case—and I think I may be typical of many

others—I didn't conduct a special search for a mentor. God drew me and my spiritual father together. We both knew deep inside ourselves, as we observed and interacted with each other over a period of years, that the relationship was right. There was a strong sense that the divine will and our human wills coincided in our friendship.

Also, there were practical, external factors that confirmed the validity of our personal tie. For one thing, I knew from his reputation that Iakovos of Derkon was a truly spiritual man, totally selfless, whose judgment and views were worth 100 percent of my attention. In fact, over the years he helped many other young people to excel in a wide variety of fields, including medicine, education, and agriculture. Only three of us who came under his spiritual influence became clergymen.

Perhaps most important of all, it was clear my spiritual father was right for me because he was always there to offer a helping hand when I needed him most. I can still recall his reaction when I came down from the pulpit, was taken to the police station, and was told in no uncertain terms that I would be forbidden to preach and teach Sunday school in Turkey. I was almost in tears over this incident because I could see that my future in Turkish territory would be seriously in jeopardy. But the blow was softened considerably because my spiritual father was there to lend a hand.

"Let's go see *another* Sunday school," he said to me.

I expected he would take me to a Protestant or Catholic Sunday school in Constantinople, where I might be able to get some new ideas about how to get around the Turkish prohibition on my activities. But instead, he took me first to a Greek Orthodox church, where we prayed together for a time. Then, we went to an apartment house, and he asked for the concierge, who lived in a small room in the basement.

As we entered these living quarters, I could see that the concierge and his family were facing hard times. His wife was sick in bed, and their son, a high school student, was a victim of tuberculosis. We first went over to the young man's bed, sat beside him, and chatted with him in an effort to cheer him up. Then, my spiritual father prayed with the boy and spent some time counseling and comforting both of the parents. Finally, he reached into his pocket and pulled out some money and some drugs that he had bought at a pharmacy for the wife.

As we walked back upstairs and headed outside, we saw that a heavy rain had just begun to fall. Neither of us had umbrellas or rain gear, and so by the time we reached our homes we were both soaked and chilled.

Just as we prepared to go our separate ways, he turned to me and asked, "How did you like the Sunday school we just visited?"

I thought of that boy we had just left, the dark and humid basement room and the prayers and conversations that had occupied us on our visit. Yes, I realized, no matter what the police said, there were plenty of ways to hold Sunday school classes in Constantinople!

I've always been drawn to stimulating intellectual discussions and readings. But through experiences like this special "Sunday school" my mentor showed me that the first priority for any Christian must be the care of and concern for other people. As he ministered to others, he displayed a humility and selflessness that always gave me something to shoot for in my own life.

Also, he never discouraged me. If I made a mistake or did something wrong, he would usually *show* me the right way to behave, rather than upbraid me verbally. More often than not, his method of instruction was to quote passages from the Old and New Testaments and then convey his opinions in a sweet, nonjudgmental way.

But still, he could be strict when he had to be. When I persisted in a mistake or in some way hurt someone—and failed to confess my wrongdoing—he would tell me in very firm language what I should do.

I can remember one time, as an eighteen-year-old student, when I complained against one of my teachers in my mentor's presence. He allowed me to say more about this other man than I should have said, and then he asked, "Are you finished?"

"Yes," I replied.

"Now, you go and ask that man's forgiveness and never come to me again to complain against your teachers," he said sternly. "First of all, you're too young to be in a position to judge your teachers. And secondly, you must remember that Jesus said, 'Don't judge, so that you may not be judged.' "

Even after I left theological school, my spiritual father kept in touch with me and continued to offer his correction and support. Unlike an ordinary teacher-student relationship, the bond between a spiritual parent and a spiritual child is a relationship that may span several periods of life—and sometimes an entire lifetime.

A teacher in school may have a tremendous impact on a young mind, an impact which lasts for years and years after graduation. But more often than not, this kind of limited influence begins to fade with time. In contrast, the relationship between a spiritual director and his charge may continue until one or the other dies. In my own case, my mentor, Archbishop Iakovos of Derkon, remained my confidant and adviser for nearly sixty years, until he died in 1982 at the age of ninety-six. I felt free to call on him at every stage in my own ministry, from my service as a priest, through my tenure as the Dean of the Cathedral and the theological school in Boston, and then on through my service as bishop and archbishop.

When I traveled to South America in 1962 and 1972, I invited him to accompany me to provide much-needed support and spiritual nurturance. Also, he was available when I found myself at the center of a political and cultural storm over the use of the Greek language in the church in the United States. At that critical time my faith and ministry might not have survived without the help of the Patriarch Athenagoras. But at the same time, I found Archbishop Iakovos of Derkon, my spiritual father, was a man on whom I could lean heavily for support.

It's hard to describe in mere words what it means to have such a spiritual mentor, who is simultaneously a guide, a firm friend, and a sharer of one's dreams. One of the miracles of the Christian experience is that a holy and edifying alliance of this type is possible between one who is young and one who is old in the faith. In some small way, I can now understand what the disciples of Christ, and also Timothy, must have enjoyed in their rich relationships with those who guided them along the inner way.

PART II

THE PRIVATE WAY

PART II

THE PRIVATE WAY

4

Pathways of Prayer

Prayer is talking to God. As a child talks to his father, so we should pray to God. During those private times, when God and I are alone together, I use simple, direct, childlike language: "I need your help again with my problems. Now, please take my hand and grant what's right."

Nothing is too small or unimportant for God's ears. After all, he knows when every sparrow falls, and he has counted all the hairs on our heads. He's concerned with the minute details of our lives. So if I have a problem, I'll take it to him and ask for help in finding the solution. I'll ask him to smooth out the differences between me and another person so that we can communicate with each other in a more loving way.

But of course, the essence of prayer is not just asking, asking, asking. Rather, it's *listening*. Early in the morning, when I first wake up, I'll sit down at my desk or in a comfortable chair with my prayer book and my Bible near at hand.

Before anything else, I'll thank God for the abundant blessings that he has given me. Then, I'll begin to meditate on those people or issues that I feel require illumination and guidance.

"Show me your way, God," I may say. Then, I'll remain silent until I experience something deep inside which cleanses my mind and my soul, something which renews me.

As I wait, I sometimes experience inner agony. My very soul hurts as I wait to hear that inner voice of God, where Jesus somehow says to me, "Come unto me."

On those occasions when I fail to hear his voice, I find I'm in pain, agonizing pain. It's not a physical pain, but an emotional and spiritual hurting, which only departs when that still small voice of God begins to get through to me.

You may ask, "What exactly is this voice? How do you know it comes from God and not only from within yourself?"

The voice I'm talking about is not an audible proclamation. It's not the type that came from heaven when Jesus was baptized, saying, "This is my beloved Son, with whom I am well pleased."*

Rather, the voice I'm referring to is closer to the "still small voice" or the "gentle breeze" that Elijah heard when he was in the cave on Mount Horeb (1 Kings 19). As Elijah listened, there was a strong wind that broke the mountain rocks into pieces, but God was not in that wind. There was also an earthquake, but God was not there either. Nor was he in a fire that swept across the mountain.

God's word to Elijah came more subtly, as a soft spring breeze may waft gently, almost imperceptibly across our faces. To hear that kind of word from God requires great sensitivity

* Matthew 3:17, RSV

and a deep relationship with him which must be cultivated for years and years.

It's my dream that one day I'll hear a clear booming voice, the kind God used when he spoke at Jesus' baptism and the Transfiguration. But for me, a typical response from God is a gentle inner nudging, or perhaps a clear, convincing word, as God speaks to me through some other human being.

So my early morning hours are devoted to the listening kind of prayer, which awaits the inner voice. When I finally sense that God is guiding me, I'll turn to other prayers and also to my Scripture readings for the day. Then, I'll eat an orange or some other piece of fruit and perhaps do some work until 7:00 or 8:00 in the morning. At that time, I'll take my shower, get dressed and prepare my breakfast. Finally, at about 9:00 or 9:30, I'm ready to face the day's regular responsibilities.

Of course, things don't always go smoothly during my encounters with God in the mornings. The pathways of private prayer can indeed be rough, with many detours and twists and turns. In fact, sometimes I don't really feel I can pray at all. I feel unworthy to pray.

Feeling unworthy to pray is mental torture for me. Sometimes, because of something I've done or said, I feel I can't approach God with a peaceful mind or heart. In effect, I deprive myself of the privilege of being in God's presence and being able to pray to him.

But I can't stay in that state for long, not if I hope to have peace and satisfaction in my life. There's a tendency when I feel this unworthiness to say, "This isn't a day when I can pray, so I'll try again tomorrow."

No! Even though I feel tempted sometimes to give in to this attitude, I know that's not what God wants. He may want some penitence, he may want some confession to him of wrongs I've committed or unloving thoughts I've harbored. He may want me to spend some time "grooming my spirit" so that I'm better able to return to a regular interaction with him. But he *doesn't* want me to hold myself off from him until tomorrow. *Today* is the time when those spiritual problems have to be resolved.

So if I don't feel capable of encountering God or communicating with him, I'll just stop for a few moments, or perhaps a half hour or an hour. I'll wait in his presence until I feel my relationship with him being restored.

Times of aridity, reluctance or blockage in prayer—the times when you feel you simply can't pray or don't want to pray—can only be dealt with through more prayer. We all feel like this at one time or another. And it's during these difficult periods, when prayer seems distasteful or meaningless, that I find meditation most helpful.

I may focus my meditation on the obvious, immediate problem: "Why don't I feel like praying? What have I done that makes me feel this way? Why do you feel so far away from me, God?"

Or I may focus on an appropriate passage of Scripture. If I'm feeling angry and my hostile emotions seem the obstacle to my prayers, I may meditate on David's words in Psalm 4:4: "Be angry, but sin not." When I've dwelt on that passage in the past, I've asked myself, what does it mean for me today? How far can I go in being angry, yet not sinning? What kind of anger did Christ have when he chased the moneychangers out of the temple?

In effect, as I discipline myself to sit down, focus on the Bible and consider such questions, I begin to reestablish my relationship with Christ, and that opens the way for productive prayer. For me, meditation is a discipline which can often lead to true prayer, or direct talking and opening of the heart before God. Meditation provides an opportunity for God's illumination in those times when I can't pray or don't know what to pray.

So the antidote for an inability to pray is more prayer and meditation. I can remember one elderly woman, a widow, who came to me early one Sunday morning for a confession while I was serving as a priest in Boston. She knelt before me and said, "I don't have a confession, but I do want to ask you a question: Why can't I pray? I simply can't seem to pray anymore!"

At the time, I was a young man, without a great deal of spiritual experience to draw upon. I couldn't think of a Bible passage, an apt theological reference, or a reasoned response to get her back on the pathway to communication with God. But what finally came to me was a suggestion that I don't believe was my own insight. Rather, I think it was direct guidance from God. All I said was, "Can we pray together?"

Our prayer together helped to open the door to a communication with God, which somehow had previously slammed shut in her life. Here, prayer itself was the pathway to prayer.

But these prayers of ours can't be sporadic, crisis-inspired "foxhole prayers," such as soldiers in combat utter when they fear they are about to be killed. The only way we can hope to develop a deep and comprehensive life of prayer and meditation is to talk regularly with God over a lifetime. Also, we can learn a great deal from others who are further along the path than we.

In any event, it's important to understand that there are no formulas. I'm sure that St. Paul, when he spent three years in the desert in Arabia, learned a great deal about the disciplines of the inner life, including private prayer. But I'm also quite certain that he didn't develop any hard-and-fast rules that could be applied to any situation. If he did, he certainly didn't pass them on to us in his writings in the Scripture!

To be sure, we have many guidelines and indications of what Paul's prayer life was like. We know it was very specific, about the many details of his life and ministry. We also know that he advocated praying constantly, thanking God in all circumstances and persevering and even agonizing in prayer. But there are no formulas. Rather, we see in Paul a remarkable sensitivity to the moving and guiding of God's spirit.

As I see Jesus praying in agony in the Garden of Gethsemane, with sweat like great drops of blood falling down on the ground . . . as I see Paul beseeching God three times to have his "thorn in the flesh" removed . . . as I see Paul, again, crying, "Wretched man that I am! Who will deliver me from this body of death?"—I know, beyond any doubt, that the life of prayer is often not easy. Yet when we stay with it and persevere until our wills are harmonious with the divine will, the rewards can be truly wonderful.

In this regard, I'm reminded of a story about a juggler who went to a monastery with the hope that the brothers inside would be able to teach him how to pray. He was told to follow the monks as they entered the chapel at certain designated hours to pray, and he did so. But still, he couldn't pray.

He tried to meditate, to read the liturgy, to emulate in every conceivable way what he saw those in the monastery doing—but all to no effect. He also recited many of the fixed prayers of the church and counted the rosary, but still, nothing worked. This juggler could not seem to break through to God.

Finally, thoroughly frustrated and ready to abandon the monastery or any further efforts at prayer, he entered the kitchen late one night, after everyone else had gone to bed. It had been a while since he had practiced his craft of juggling, and he felt a gnawing need to perform. So he got a load of dishes, took them outside to a part of the chapel which contained a statue of the Virgin Mary and began to toss the plates in the air, juggling them on and on into the night.

Finally, after an hour or more of this vigorous physical activity, he fell to his knees, thoroughly exhausted, before the statue of the Virgin. At that moment, so the story goes, the statue came to life, took the edge of her garment and wiped the sweat from his forehead.

In this way, the juggler finally discovered how to pray. Without really knowing what he was doing, he prayed in the only way that he really knew. He directed all his physical and mental faculties as a juggler toward God until, physically, emotionally, and spiritually, he was literally at the end of his rope. He could go on no further, and at that very moment, God responded to him.

In short, the juggler approached God honestly and transparently. He relied not on false language or emotions, but on the simple, unadorned offering of his entire self to God. By using the best means of communication available to him—his juggling—he found the doorway opened to a more in-depth dialogue with God.

The former chaplain of the U.S. Senate, Peter Marshall, remarked one time that prayer can be especially dangerous for people who pray falsely. For example, when we pray, "Our Father who art in heaven," it's absolutely essential for us to approach God as truly our father and to assume before him the attitude of the child. Entering God's presence in any other way involves treachery, because we are refusing to accept him on his terms. Also, in our human weakness, we in effect try to hide our real selves from him.

The juggler did just the opposite. He approached God simply and honestly, with great perseverance, and God honored his seriousness. Similarly, if we approach God just as we are, without any tricks, deception, or false fronts, he'll respond positively. And the way will be open to a meaningful relationship in prayer.

In short, the model for powerful and effective prayer is an intensely personal model. You can't hope to talk freely and constructively with a human friend unless you're honest and open with that person and build a solid relationship with him over a period of years. It's the same way with God.

At times, the pathway of prayer may seem to be primarily an uphill climb, with few exhilarating vistas or energizing breaths of clear mountain air. But eventually, those who stick with this spiritual discipline find that private prayer is one of the most important avenues of God's grace in their lives. As we reach out to him and show him our seriousness, he responds, though often in ways that we don't anticipate. And in those moments—as when the virgin came alive for the juggler—we begin to experience the full range of God's relationship with us, from hearing the still, small voice, to witnessing genuine miracles in our daily lives.

5

The Fundamentals
of Faith

Faith is not something that can be taught. Rather, true faith develops over years and decades as we pursue our personal life with God.

To put this another way, the knowledge of God arises from the experience of a firm faith. Faith comes before knowledge, not the other way around. In the spiritual realm, it won't do just to get dozens of theological books from the library and spend all your time studying them. In short, you can't really know God unless you're a believer.

Certainly, once your faith is in place, knowledge can help provide a fuller understanding of who God is and how he works in this world. Also, knowledge can serve as a kind of "lawyer," which will justify or condemn your actions, your failures and your faults. But knowledge can't save you. Knowledge can't bring you into the presence of God. Only faith, as the channel of God's grace, can do that.

So faith is not a matter merely of the intellect or brain power—nor is it limited to church liturgy or ritual, or to intense emotions felt in a particular worship service. To be sure, the liturgy is a wonderful and essential part of worship, and a stirring sermon or soaring song can help the human spirit take flight. But too often, individual worshipers assume that they have an adequate relationship with God—and an adequate faith—if they only appear in church for regular services or follow their church prayer book closely.

A genuine experience of faith, in contrast, has to take us on spiritual journeys far beyond the printed pages that we read or songs and sermons in services every Sunday. True faith is a matter not of outward form, regardless of how beautiful or exciting it may be. Rather, faith is rooted in one's inner being and identity.

Certainly, theological knowledge, the church liturgy, and worship services can provide us with many of the keys to faith and spiritual growth. After all, valid theologies and liturgies are based on spiritual truth, and the more we expose ourselves to such influences, the closer we move toward an understanding of that truth.

Yet in the last analysis, what is ultimate truth if not Jesus himself? You'll recall that he said, "*I* am the truth. . . ."

So suppose a person says to me, "I really want to have faith—can you show me how?" My best answer to this question is, "If you want faith, follow Jesus."

Faith involves a deep inner experience of trust with the Savior. As such, the "walk" of faith, as St. Paul puts it, involves one's whole deportment and attitude toward life. That's why it's not enough to rely on the intellect alone, as in theological study, or on the voice alone, as in reciting the liturgy, or one's presence alone, as in attending services. Rather, faith must grasp the entire person—the heart and the will as well as the intellect and the outer trappings of our lives.

How does faith begin? It begins deep inside us, in our personal response to Christ. He calls to us, and we decide to follow. From that very personal and private beginning, faith grows day by day, year by year, until it permeates every part of our beings.

Also, faith links us intimately with other believers, just as it links us to Christ. And a developed faith gives us assurance and confidence in our fervent hope for the fulfillment of God's promises—an assurance which enables us to reach out and love those in the world around us.

Clearly, then, faith is not something we "have" or "acquire," as a result of learning or affirming some doctrinal statement or performing some ritual. Rather, our faith reflects who and what we really are as human beings. So if I hear someone say, as I often have, "I lost my faith during such and such a period in my life," I don't think they've lost their faith at all. I think they've lost themselves.

In my own life, I've sensed that my faith has wavered at times when I have asked God for something and he hasn't given it to me in quite the way I expected. Yet I know now it isn't so much my faith that wavers as my very being, my fundamental sense of who I am and what my purpose should be in this world.

Back in 1934, when I really wanted to go to graduate school at the Sorbonne and study philosophy, I kept beseeching God, asking him to do what I felt was his will for my life and my studies. When it seemed that I wouldn't be able to pursue quite the course of graduate study I had wanted, I pleaded with God: "All I want is to have a better opportunity to serve you in the future!"

And God's answer? Silence. Complete silence.

I soon came to realize that there was a basic conflict between my will and his will. At first on that occasion, I sensed my faith had been shaken. I worried that I simply didn't have enough faith to cause God to respond to me in the way that I wanted. But that was my very problem: I was focusing too much on what *I* wanted, rather than on what God wanted. Faith, I thought, was a vehicle for moving God in my preconceived direction, rather than opening me to his guidance.

That attitude wasn't true faith, of course, but just another expression of my own human will. Before long, as I stood before God, I found that my entire identity as a person with certain ambitions and goals was being called into question. For a time, I lost myself, in the sense that I lost my direction in life and my perception of God's will.

But faith, as the means of bringing my will into conformity with his, was always present, always a possibility. I just didn't know how to take advantage of the opportunities available to me. Then, I began to focus more closely on those practices and principles that build up faith: I prayed; I consulted with my spiritual mentors; and I sought God's will. Finally I understood that my personal academic ambitions were not quite what God had in mind for me. At the same time, my faith in his concern and intentions for my future grew. In a small but important way, I had learned to accept the fact that my personal will might not always coincide at first with God's divine will.

Jesus showed us the way to this kind of faith when he wrestled in prayer in the Garden of Gethsemane. As he asked the Father to remove the cup of death from him, a great tension arose between his humanity and his divinity. But then, in the same breath, he said, "Nevertheless not my will, but thine, be done."

Here, Jesus subjected his humanity to his divinity. He fought the natural inclinations of his human nature to save himself and avoid pain and separation from the Father—and he won. He chose what was right for him; what is best for us; and what conformed most perfectly to the will of the Father. He chose to die so that an alienated world might be reconciled to God.

Even as I confront my own relatively minor problems, it's comforting for me to recall that Jesus himself, as well as many of the early leaders of the church, wrestled with difficult issues of faith, trust, and conformity to the Father's will. One of the most difficult moments—and crises of faith—that I have faced as an archbishop occurred in 1970, when I presented my views on the use of language in the Greek Orthodox Church in America.

I felt strongly that the church should use two languages in the United States, both Greek and English, with emphasis on more English. But when I went public with my views, I immediately encountered tremendous opposition from those who wanted to keep a primary emphasis on the use of Greek. Thousands of recent immigrants and ardent devotees of the Greek language collected signatures against me and my position, and they sent them in protest to the Patriarch and to Greece. Many of these petitions even demanded that I be forced to resign. It seemed for a time that I was standing alone, as even the Greek-speaking press took sides against me.

Then came the most devastating blow of all: The Patriarch in Constantinople responded to my opponents that "the language in which the Gospels were written must be preserved." That seemed to be just the word that my critics wanted to hear as a first step to defeat my position and terminate my ministry.

When I learned of the response of the Patriarch, it certainly seemed that he had allied himself with those who were attacking me. My immediate response was, "What's the use?" For two entire days and nights, I "lost myself" in a profoundly disturbing way that I've never experienced before or since. I also thought I might be losing my faith. Had I completely lost the way to God's will? Was I now incapable of leading the flock over which I believed he had placed me?

But even though I wasn't entirely aware of it, my faith was still there. I know that now, despite the fact that I was having great difficulty sorting through my own conflicting emotions. If I had lacked faith entirely, I'm sure I would have sent a telegram immediately to the Patriarch with my resignation. But instead, I waited, hoping to hear some word from the Lord.

As it happened, waiting on God was a very good thing to do. Just before I sat down to write my letter of resignation to the Patriarch, I received a note from his chief secretary, who spoke for the Patriarch himself. The note said, "Don't doubt for a moment the understanding and the compassion and the love of the Patriarch for you."

That was exactly what I needed to hear to be able to persevere in the face of the challenges from those who accused me of trying to de-Hellenize the church and its people. Now, I knew for a certainty that I didn't stand alone.

Of course, I had always known that God was with me, and my intention was to serve his people as best I could. But sometimes, as we've seen, the human will and the divine will can get confounded. At the outset, I had thought I was on the right track as I was promoting the adequate understanding and living of the faith.

Although my commitment was to the Greek Orthodox Church in America, I began to question my own wisdom and judgment: Was I expressing God's will or a grandiose plan of my own? Had I received a word from God that would enhance the future of the Gospel in the Western Hemisphere? Or was I acting "after the rudiments of the world"? (Colossians 2:8, KJV)

With the encouraging and supportive word from my Patriarch, Athenagoras, the answer to these questions became clear. As a result, I became more confident, my doubts faded, and strength was restored to my waning faith. In this case, as in all others, my faith in a provident God was integrally wrapped up in who I was as a human being.

Faith, then, lies at the very foundation of our personal relationship with God. As such, faith is a necessary prerequisite, an absolute *sine qua non* of effective communication with God. As Jesus said in Matthew 21:22, "And whatever you ask in prayer, you will receive, if you have faith." In fact, without faith, we know from the Scripture, it's impossible to know God's will for us.

On the other hand, faith is not all there is to the Christian life. Even that great exponent of faith, St. Paul—who proclaimed that we're justified and saved through faith—placed faith below love in God's hierarchy of virtues. In writing to the church at Corinth, he said that faith, hope, and love abide, but "the greatest of these is love."

Yet when God's love is present, faith is the key that unlocks the doors of the spiritual life, including the basic relationship with Jesus. To become his children, we first need faith in the sense that we have to believe *in* him or *on* him. Those little words, "in" and "on"—the Greek words *eis* and *epi*—imply much more than intellectual assent. They suggest submission to Christ as a person, a decision to enter into an ongoing, all-encompassing relationship with him.

Faith, in its fundamental and most powerful form, is to unquestioningly and committedly "follow Jesus."

6

What Is Adoration?

Among those who are serious about their faith we hear a great deal these days about the adoration of God. There are "songs of adoration"; there is "adoration of the host," or blessed sacrament; there are "prayers of adoration." In one popular formulation, complete prayer should include four major parts, represented by the acronym ACTS: Adoration, Confession, Thanksgiving, and Supplication.

Yet what *is* adoration?

For those who like succinct, neat definitions, you might say adoration is the supreme form of love that a human being can give to God. And to be sure, that's an accurate enough definition of the word. But to understand adoration fully, to experience it in the depths of our beings, it's necessary to go beyond mere words.

Any understanding of adoration must begin with an understanding of love. Yet love—like its highest expression, adoration—is also something that is very difficult, if not impossible, to qualify or encompass in human language.

Consider for a moment just how inadequate words can be. In English, we have just one word, "love," which is supposed to apply to a wide variety of feelings and relationships. So we say, "I love my child . . . I love my spouse . . . I love my friend . . . I love God," and even, "I love my new shoes!"

In the Greek, there are several words that help us to say "I love" in somewhat more precise terms. One of these words, *eros,* refers to the most intense feelings of human physical love between the sexes. Another word, *philia,* is used for the love of friendship, or brotherly love, as the term is used in 2 Peter 1:7.

The highest, noblest form of love is the love of God, a love that carries the name *agape* in the New Testament. This is the kind of love that St. John attributes to God when he wrote in his Gospel, "For God so loved the world that he gave his only begotten son. . . ." Also, this *agape* love is a love that God empowers us as human beings to show and share with others and also with him. It's the same love St. Paul refers to as the greatest virtue in his first letter to the Corinthians.

But even though the Greek is more precise than English in describing love, words can only take us so far. I would never try to wrap up any form of love, and especially *agape* love, into a neat verbal package. True love is something I must *feel*— either emanating from God, from another human being, or from myself. That's the only way I can know that divine love really exists and that it's operative in a given situation.

The ability to love is a very rare human quality, and when it's present in a person, you know it. You don't have to ask; it's just there, for you to enjoy and experience. I know I've encountered a person who loves when his or her face seems so clear that a kind of light projects from inside, shining clearly on me and on others. I always revel in meeting such people, because I invariably leave their presence feeling uplifted. Also, I find that this ability to love may be present in people of all ages, whether children, adolescents or those who are middle-aged and older. Unfortunately, though, I haven't met too many people who emanate *agape* love.

Who have I met with this ability to love? The majority have been people whom you wouldn't know. But let me mention a few that you *do* know. President Dwight Eisenhower was such a man. So is former President Jimmy Carter. Also, Secretary of State George Shultz is a man in whom the light of love clearly shines forth.

I've always felt comfortable in meetings with Secretary Shultz. In one recent meeting I particularly noticed that the conversation and also the nonverbal communication between us flowed back and forth so beautifully, so eloquently. I didn't experience a bit of difficulty in expressing myself, and the lulls or moments of silence we experienced were natural and comfortable.

It made no difference to me what Secretary Shultz's political views on a given issue were, whether he was liberal or conservative. It didn't even matter whether or not he was a good Secretary of State or what religious denomination he belonged to. The important thing was that there was a kind of transparency about him. A light inside him shone forth through his eyes and fell upon me, a light which immediately warmed my heart and our relationship.

In part, this feeling of warmth and ease in an encounter with another person can be just a matter of personal style. I remember once that the late President Truman told me he had recently been in touch with three leading clergymen.

"Two of them I have always loved and respected, but one I've never liked," he said to me.

"Why, Mr. President?" I asked.

"Because when that man talks to me, he doesn't look in my eyes," President Truman said.

Certainly, some shy or reserved people find it hard to look into the eyes of another person, and that's quite understandable. But shy or not—and regardless of individual styles of expression and social skills—I've found that a person who really has the capacity, the *agape* capacity, to love others will communicate that love in a transparent way through the eyes. The shyness in his personality may still be there and may make him more deferential and reserved than another person. But still, the love comes through.

All this is just a very human, down-to-earth way of suggesting what the love of God is all about. God offers his love to us in a direct, warm, caring beam of divine light. His love streams directly from his heart to ours. All we need do is receive, in order to enjoy it fully and bask in its comforting rays.

But for us to receive God's love in its fullness, we must have a genuine relationship with him in our innermost beings. It's essential that we in some sense be in union with him as a result of a decision to love, trust, and follow his Son. Then, when we've established and developed such a relationship, we find that we, in turn, can become human channels for the great and powerful *agape* love that we've received from God. We can return love to him, and we can also express this same love to others, in much the same way God has expressed it to us. As St. John says in his first epistle, "We love, because he first loved us."

This understanding of love also applies to adoration because, as I've said, adoration is the supreme love that a living person can give to God. Yet adoration, like love, is a word that is frequently abused. We talk about adoring an article of clothing in the same language that we talk about adoring God. Yet how different and special the adoration of God is!

Adoration arises naturally from our personal communication with God and is a supreme expression of our belief and trust in him. If you adore God, that means you have placed all your hopes in him. You believe that he is the source of all love. You also trust that he will communicate his will to you because you have indisputable evidence of his great love, a love that he expressed in the willing sacrifice of his Son for you personally.

But adoring God is not just a matter of saying "I adore you" or "I love you." In fact, I myself have never said, "God, I love you," or "God, I adore you." For me, that would be mocking God.

Others, of course, might feel more comfortable adoring God in this way. In fact, many children can easily say, "I love you so much" to a parent—and they really mean it! For that matter, the parent likes to hear words like these. And certainly, our Heavenly Father will honor simple, heartfelt expressions of affection if he receives them from his children and if they show they mean it through their acts.

But such language, no matter how sincere, has its limits. Even if we begin with simple statements of love or adoration, we must eventually reach beyond them. On a personal level, in my own private prayer times, I remain convinced that God knows very well the depth of my soul and my spirit, and he understands better than I whether I love him or adore him. His Spirit penetrates my entire life and being—even my kidney functions, as the Bible says. In the Scriptures, the kidneys, heart, and liver were regarded as the centers of human sensation, passion, love and hatred. So to plumb our depths, God must examine every part of us, including even the kidneys!

I also know that as God explores the most secret parts of my body and being, he knows it would be inadequate for me just to say to him, "I love you." Instead, I must be more specific. I must think more in terms of what St. Paul said in the eighth chapter of his Epistle to the Romans, where he wrote that powerful and very specific passage of adoration:

> For I am sure that neither death, nor life, nor angels, nor principalities, nor things present, nor things to come, nor powers, nor height, nor depth, nor anything else in all creation, will be able to separate us from the love of God in Christ Jesus our Lord.

In addition to requiring such specificity, a genuine adoration of God also requires service and commitment, both to God and to others. I've always been fascinated by Jesus' response to Peter in the last chapter of John's Gospel.

You'll recall that Jesus asked Peter, "Do you love me more than these?"

Peter answered "Yes, Lord; you know that I love you."

And Jesus replied, "Feed my lambs."

Jesus then asked Peter a second time, "Do you love me?" Again, Peter replied that he did, and once more, Jesus told him to take care of his sheep.

The third time Jesus asked the question, Peter seemed to get a little disturbed or even annoyed. Perhaps it appeared to this dynamic disciple that his Master wasn't accepting his answers at face value. Yet Jesus was just trying to emphasize an important point. He wanted to make it clear that words were not enough in the expression of love or adoration. Rather, it was also necessary for Peter to *act*—to feed and protect the sheep of Christ's flock, even at the risk of Peter's own life.

Peter's responsibilities were weighty, and they would eventually lead him to die for the cause of Christ. His adoration of Christ obviously had to go far beyond the words "I love you." In his case—and the same should be true in ours—adoration found its ultimate expression in complete submission and obedience to the will of God.

Clearly, the adoration of God is a profound and complex experience. As the supreme expression of belief and trust, it's not an attitude or prayer style that can come to you overnight through a kind of magic transformation. Rather, the ability to adore God, to love him fully and completely, is a quality that must be cultivated over a period of years, in the deepest recesses of the soul, spirit, and mind. When you truly adore God, you go beyond mere words to a full offering of your life to him. You deliver yourself into his hands, where he can do with you as he wills.

Imagine taking such a step with another human being: Suppose you put yourself totally under the control of a particular person and agreed to allow that person to direct your life according to his will, rather than yours. That would take a great deal of trust wouldn't it? It would take so much trust in the other person that few of us would ever be willing to do this on a human level. In fact, we *shouldn't* do it!

To put yourself completely in the hands and under the power of another person involves an assumption that this other person is truly trustworthy, truly able to direct your life better than you or anyone else can. Do you know any human being who is so perfect that he or she deserves this responsibility over your life? I certainly don't.

Yet I do know one Person, God himself, who *is* trustworthy. He is worthy, as no one else, of our total allegiance. He is worthy to be master of our lives. He is worthy of our supreme love—indeed, of our adoration.

7

Explosive Worship

Sometimes, modern people have trouble "getting into" a traditional worship service. By this, I mean they can't see that the experience has any relevance or meaning for them personally.

For example, if a person is really honest, he might admit: "I get bored with Sunday services."

Or: "The singing and preaching I hear are poor entertainment, compared with what I can get at a local rock concert, in the movies, or on television."

Or: "I attend services fairly regularly, but frankly, I can take them or leave them. The experience is rather 'flat' for me because I don't get very much out of it."

Unfortunately, these and other such negative attitudes are widespread these days in many denominations. But why is this? Who is at fault?

At least in part, the fault lies with the clergy and others

who organize and present the services. We don't always make it easy for lay people to get inspired by the Sunday morning worship experience. There are many reasons.

- The liturgy may be presented in a perfunctory manner;
- Songs may be played and sung with very little life or exuberance; or
- Sermons may be too academic and pedantic on the one hand, or poorly prepared on the other.

Still, the leaders of our services shouldn't bear all the blame for the failure of worship. On the contrary, this failure can also be traced to the attitudes of lay people. Too often, those sitting in the pews come to Sunday worship poorly prepared. Also, they come with the wrong expectations.

But what do I mean here? How can you get prepared for worship, or develop the right expectations? Most important of all, how can a lay person experience enthusiastic, life-changing, and even "explosive" worship, as I sometimes call it?

To answer these questions, let's first spend some time exploring how to prepare for the experience. Then, you may find that your expectations about what God can do for you and with you in church begin to change. And with such change, your boredom will turn to fascination; your feelings of flatness to exuberant enthusiasm.

I regard worship as an exultation of the human spirit—so much so that at certain times, a total separation of my spirit from my body seems to take place. At the most intense moments of worship, I feel that I've been ushered into another realm of existence, much as the poets say they experience. My spirit and soul enter such a state that I seem actually to go out of this world. At those times, I can't always tell you whether I'm standing on the floor of the church or floating above it!

Because of the powerful influence of worship in my life, I like to use the word "enthusiasm" to characterize my feelings. This term comes from a Greek word that means "God is in you." A truly enthusiastic person is one who experiences the presence of God within—to the extent that the person may become so exuberant and exultant that he feels he's about to explode.

I suspect that one of the main functions of singing in the church is to act as a channel for this explosive power. Sometimes, I feel the presence of God so intensely that I sense my entire being is about to blow to bits. On those occasions, I have to find some physical release. And "roof-raising" song is the best way to unleash the powerful spiritual dynamite—or concentrated *dynamis,* to use the Greek—welling up within me.

Yet obviously, not everyone is as positive about worship as I am. And as I've indicated, a major reason that many people feel bored or "out of it" when they come into a worship service is that they haven't prepared themselves beforehand for this particular experience with God. Remember some of the things we've said about faith, adoration, and other expressions of spirituality. As you know, it's impossible to love God completely, to adore him, to have faith in him, without first establishing a relationship with him. Love, faith, and adoration only become meaningful when they arise out of a deep, ongoing commitment to Christ.

Similarly, true worship can only arise from such a personal relationship with God. But even if you have such a relationship with Christ, you may still find that you don't get a great deal out of a typical worship service. If that's the case, the reason could be that your expectations are unrealistic or improper in some way.

One of the most common problems that people face these days is that when they gather together socially to witness some presentation on a platform or stage, they expect to be *entertained*. They look forward to exciting, modern music executed with a high degree of skill . . . or a stream of well-prepared jokes . . . or a thrilling recreation of a car chase or other cliff-hanging event. Highly professional, expert entertainers on TV and in the movies can grab our interest and hold it for a spine-tingling hour or so—and we expect the same thing of those leading a worship service.

Unfortunately, these expectations are completely misplaced. To be effective and moving, the worship experience must be primarily *participatory*. In other words, we shouldn't go to church in order to be entertained; we must enter the sanctuary with the idea that we'll join with others in the giving of ourselves to God. Worship, in fact, implies a supreme form of serving and honoring God. In a sense, *he* is the audience, and we are the ones who should be "putting on the show." For the Christian, expressing such honor or service to God can best be done through the total offering of the self to God. And worship services provide us with regular opportunities to do just that.

So when we have a relationship with God and our expectations are right, we're more likely to find ourselves poised for an exhilarating and even explosive worship experience. If I may speak personally, whenever I've entered a worship service and these two factors have been operative in my own life, I've never felt bored; I've never wished I were somewhere else. Instead, I've found that the service reflects a special divine light on me. Through the songs, the passages of Scripture, and the words of those who preach and lead the celebration, Christ acts to deepen my relationship with him.

When I'm in such a mood, I often find that the familiar words of worship take on new and inspiring meanings. For example, I have read or heard many times the words of St. Paul to the Galatians, "I have been crucified with Christ."

At first, when I heard those words, I approached them intellectually and simplistically. I thought that my life would automatically and quickly become like the life of the Crucified, once I had begun a relationship with him.

But as time has gone by and I have considered those words again in subsequent times of worship, I have discovered that I see things differently. I can no longer say glibly that "I am crucified with God." Certainly, I don't lead a "crucified" life in the sense that Jesus did. I don't have that kind of faith, love, adoration, trust. I don't have that kind of identity.

Also, as I move on in that same passage in Paul's Letter to the Galatians, I read, "It is no longer I who live, but Christ who lives in me." Again, from one era of my life to the next, I've found I've heard different messages from these identical words.

In my youth, I thought it was a very simple thing to see that I was alive and able to go on living because somebody else, namely the Son of God, had died for me. Now, I still see that; but I also see something else. I live today because I receive a continual transfusion of life from Christ. The life in Christ is an ongoing experience which intensifies day by day as I draw closer to him.

Also, I find as I grow older that I become much more aware of my faults and shortcomings. I realize that even though Christ does live in me, he could live in me much more fully if I would give myself to him more completely in prayer and meditation. He is calling me to do more to make my life his life.

The more I consider such words from St. Paul during a worship experience, the more I realize that nothing in the Christian life is static or unchanging. Everything continues to grow, to move forward, to be challenged. If I ever enter a worship experience without feeling this challenge, this sense of dynamic movement and power, I always know that somehow I haven't prepared myself or approached God with the proper expectations.

These, then, are a few personal observations on the nature of worship, and especially that kind of worship which involves such closeness to God that it makes us feel as though we're about to explode from within. To understand these concepts more fully, however, it's helpful to consider in more specific terms the impact of the liturgy of the church, especially as the liturgy moves toward its ultimate culmination during Holy Week and Easter.

8

Christ in the Liturgy

When I enter a church to participate in worship, the liturgy, the order of worship, ushers me in a mystical way into the very life of Christ.

During the course of a year in our church, the divine liturgy reenacts the life of Jesus, from the day of his birth to the day of his ascent into heaven. So anytime I join in a worship service, I am also joining in the flow of the Savior's life, a flow that washes up in a high mystical wave as worshipers kneel down to pray and take Communion.

A person coming into only one isolated church service may miss this divine flow of the Spirit. So the entire experience may seem to be "dead" or meaningless, at least at first. After all, a person who is unfamiliar with the historical events in the life of Christ, or unfamiliar with a particular religious tradition, will always require some time to begin to *feel* these things in the depths of his soul.

If you've had trouble seeing the relevance of worship, my advice is this: Take some time to get accustomed to the liturgy. Attend worship services every Sunday for awhile, and try to listen to what God is saying to you during those times. I find that those Christians who do attend Sunday worship services regularly are more inclined to have a gleam in their faces, a look of great contentment and emotional satisfaction, when they leave for their homes. They have listened closely, and God has spoken to them.

As I look into the faces of those who are participating regularly in worship, I see an important spiritual event taking place in them, beginning with the doxology. Then, they get more and more involved as we proceed to the reading of the Epistles and the Gospel. In many, a mood of mystical identification with Christ, along with emotional exultation, begins to build as we proceed toward the end of the service. Finally, we join in singing the enthusiastic exclamatory hymn, "May the Name of the Lord Be Blessed Now and Forever." At that time, God uses the worship service to put a finishing touch on the souls and hearts of the faithful.

I'm especially impressed with the experience of the faithful worshiper on ordinary Sundays, rather than on the great holidays such as Christmas or Easter. In many ways, I enjoy the services of the average Sunday more than I do those of special occasions. Why? I think people who are participating regularly tend to be caught up more in the flow of the liturgy as a *lived* experience, rather than just a spectacular event to be observed.

Of course, even though ordinary Sunday services are the "staple" of spiritual development through worship, the Holy Week leading up to Easter is a very special time for me. During that entire week, I often experience what seems like constant communication with God. He is very much present, very much alive in my life, always talking with me and drawing me more and more into himself. As he suffers, I suffer. As he triumphs over evil and death, so do I.

Yet I find I must prepare myself if I hope to get the most out of this special time. So during Holy Week, I separate myself from the everyday cares of my life. I don't have office hours; I don't receive calls. My entire mind and being center on how I can best participate in the liturgy, how I can live the life of Christ every hour.

Sometimes, as I look back on the more than fifty years I've spent serving the church, I think that perhaps I wouldn't still be living today if Holy Week hadn't been there to sustain me. For me, those seven days encourage genuine renewal, genuine revival. During that short period, it doesn't matter to me if I eat or drink. My only concern is to join with fellow believers so that we can worship God in a special and powerful way together.

But unlike many other people, I feel the presence of God most deeply on Holy Saturday, the day before Easter, rather than on Easter Sunday itself. There's a tremendous sense of anticipation as we gather together late on Saturday night and wait for the stroke of midnight, which ushers in Easter itself.

Everyone waits solemnly and expectantly because they know Christ is still in the grave, still in that state of death that he chose so that we might live. Thousands of people wait.

During the liturgy on Holy Saturday, there is a time when I exclaim to the people, *"Anastao Theos!"*—"Rise from the dead, oh God!" At that point, I can't hold back my tears. In a sense, at that moment I partake in Christ's anguish over the world. Yet like my fellow worshipers, I wait with supreme anticipation. I want him to come forth for the salvation of all.

Gradually, as midnight nears, thousands of people crowd into the cathedral, holding their tapers, or candles, and waiting for the moment when Christ will come forth. The liturgy, the story of his death and resurrection, is so real to true believers that they can actually *feel* his presence in the tomb. They can hardly contain themselves with the approach of that pregnant moment when the stone is finally rolled away and he comes forth.

Finally, the time arrives. I say, *"Christos anesti!"*— "Christ is risen!" And everyone in my hearing cries with one voice, thousands upon thousands of them, "Indeed, he is risen!"

It's a joyous moment, filled with happy tears, beaming smiles, festive gestures—like the cracking of colored hard-boiled eggs to show that the tomb is now truly open. Then, many return to their homes, still holding their tapers, and they make the sign of the cross on the upper part of their doors before they enter.

In the cathedral, we continue with the Divine Liturgy, the story of Jesus' resurrection experiences. Many of those who are the most deeply committed and who experience the most moving, ongoing encounters with God's Spirit are those who remain to participate in this Divine Liturgy. Although the resurrection event is celebrated more dramatically, the abiding light of Christ may shine even more brightly among those who stay for the quieter, later services.

My mother was one of those people who was always there, listening to every word of the entire Divine Liturgy. Even though she was not an educated woman, she knew the liturgy by heart. On many occasions, I heard her quote at length from the liturgical readings, the Epistles and the Gospels. And she wasn't alone in this ability. Many others in our neighborhood and in nearby villages could quote from the Divine Liturgy at will: The words had become an integral part of their beings and exerted a lasting impact on their lives.

So, clearly, those who immerse themselves in the form of the religious service don't become imprisoned by that form. Rather, they are freed to live the Christian life with a consistency that would not otherwise be possible. In short, a deep understanding and experience of the liturgy influences the way we think and the way we live, including our morality and the quality of our relationships with others.

Also, becoming thoroughly immersed in the words of the worship service and the words of Scripture sets the stage to allow the human spirit to soar. A familiarity with the liturgy is a means to break free of the shackles of logical, rational thought and to move up to the intuitive, mystical mountaintops of the Spirit.

When I use the term "mysticism," by the way, I'm not referring to some strange, other-worldly experience available only to the few. Rather, mysticism suggests a special state of the mind and heart that enables you to become completely detached from your daily preoccupations. This feeling may last only for a few moments. But when it does occur, you know, without being able to offer any logical explanations, that somehow you have entered God's presence in a special way.

Also, those who embark on these mystical flights enjoy them immensely! I especially savor participating in the worship services because I never know when that mystical uplifting may come upon me and provide me with a sense of lightness and extra energy. St. Paul, in his Second Letter to the Corinthians, briefly described a very dramatic experience of this type when he said that he had "entered the 'third heaven'" and "heard things that cannot be told, which man may not utter."

Paul's mystical experience took him to a peak that most of us will never see. Still, we can all experience this union with God to one degree or another if we'll just prepare ourselves for it. How do we prepare? This kind of mysticism is not some sort of manufactured illusion or self-inspired daydreaming. It's an experience that arises from regular contact with God, both in the liturgy and in our private spiritual disciplines.

Even if I never see St. Paul's third heaven, I thank God that I have been given at least a taste of that special union. Without such intimate encounters, my life would be terribly empty. Yet with them, I think I get a sample, even if a small one, of what union with Christ in heaven must be like.

9

The Well of Scripture

I often think of the Scripture as a well, a repository of the living water Jesus described to the Samaritan woman in St. John's Gospel.

Consider a few of the connections: You can't get all the liquid you need to sustain you over a lifetime from one drink of well water. Similarly, you can't get all you need for a lifetime of spiritual growth from just one reading of a scriptural passage. Rather, you must keep coming back for more, keep refreshing yourself, not only to survive but also to have the energy and alertness you need to accomplish God's will as he reveals it to you.

Also, it goes without saying that a well is not a glass of water! That is, you can't just tip the well, as you do the glass, and have a quick drink. An old-fashioned well requires some work. You have to lower the bucket down deep in the shaft and allow it to fill up with that cool, pure well water. Then, you must raise the bucket up, foot by foot, until your drink is within your grasp.

Similarly, getting the maximum amount of living water out of the Scriptures requires some effort. For those with little or no background in the Bible, the first days and even weeks of study may be almost painful. A beginner may read over a strange passage several times and even listen for several hours to a competent teacher. Yet he may still not understand fully what the words mean and how they can be applied to his life.

But the serious spiritual pilgrim, who is determined to move forward and seize the prizes that are possible in the Christian life, can expect some significant rewards from Bible study. Any honest effort with the Scriptures will eventually bear fruit. And that fruit will probably arrive much sooner than you expect!

Still, it's quite painful for me to look out over almost any congregation in America as the typical preacher tries to expound the meaning of the Bible. Why painful? More often than not, I *never* see Bibles in the hands of those in the congregation who are listening to the speaker. Most people rarely seem to use the Bible for reference, even when preachers encourage them to do so.

You might say, "Well, maybe those lay people just forgot their Bibles. Or maybe they don't even own a Bible—why not give them one?"

Many churches have tried that, including our own. Some place Bibles in their pews; others award Bibles to members of the congregation on special occasions. In our own Greek Orthodox Church, we have often given Sunday School children Bibles of their own. Our hope, of course, is that they will begin to read them and become more acquainted with the contents of Scripture as they grow older.

Generally speaking, though, I don't think it works just to hand out Bibles to people. Instead, they must develop the motivation to read and study on their own on a regular basis. Occasional, cursory readings won't do the job, just as a spoonful of water won't save a person who is dying of thirst. In fact, as far as the Bible is concerned, I think that a little Bible reading may be worse than none at all.

I can recall one man who read in the Scriptures for the first time Jesus' words, "Love your enemies." This seemed like a fine idea to him because he had a particular enemy who was giving him many problems in the business where he worked. As he saw it, "loving" his nemesis in rather superficial terms should quickly solve all the problems in their relationship.

So without so much as a second thought, much less a prayer, he approached his adversary the next day with very little subtlety or sensitivity. He had no comprehension of what "love your enemies" really means or how that principle should be applied in real-life situations. Among other things, he began to do all sorts of inappropriate favors for the man, and he frequently told the fellow how much he liked him.

In fact, I understand that at one point he actually said, "You know, I really have to say I *love* you!"

On one level, you have to admire this man's willingness to take Jesus' words in the Bible seriously enough to change his actions. Also, loving an enemy in the biblical sense usually does require some risks, some bold initiatives on the part of the Christian who is trying to repair a relationship. And this individual was certainly willing to take risks! But such risks should only be taken under the guidance of God's Spirit, after considerable prayer and preparation—and usually under the guidance of a spiritual mentor or other more experienced believers.

Obviously, then, this "loving" man didn't really understand what he was doing. In effect, he attempted to apply a biblical principle in almost a magical fashion. Moreover, he neglected to do the most important thing, something he should have done at the very outset: He failed to spend time in prayer and to ask God's Spirit to guide him and sensitize him in restructuring his relationship with his colleague.

An experience like this confirms for me that we need the Bible desperately; we need the living water that this spiritual well contains. In fact, we can't function and grow properly without the well water of scriptural truth. Yet if we approach the Scriptures haphazardly or unwisely, we may find ourselves even worse off than when we began. So what's the wisest way to approach the Bible?

First of all, it's important to put God in charge by praying each time before you read or study the Bible. In our own liturgy, there's a beautiful prayer that precedes the reading of the Scriptural lessons for the day: "Illumine our eyes with the ability to capture thy divine wisdom for the words we are about to hear." God's Spirit is our first and most important guide. He should be leading us as we prepare to explore words that have been divinely inspired.

Next, as adults we should recognize that religion is not like most other subjects that are taught in a classroom. Rather, spiritual truth, whether from the Scriptures or from other texts, must be transmitted or communicated from the heart, rather than just taught as a purely intellectual concept.

So to understand the Scripture properly and to be able to use it effectively, you have to begin with a special sort of teacher. Clearly, the teacher can't just be one who is well-versed in the theological, historical, and other scholarly aspects of the Bible. Of course, I would be a relatively superficial student of the Bible without the training I received in my school of theology. But ironically, that knowledge by itself has contributed little or nothing to my understanding of God or my relationship with him. The key influence on my growth has been the personal faith of my teachers. Only those who truly believed and practiced what they taught had a profound impact on me.

The first and perhaps the most important of my teachers, one who never had any connection with a school of theology, was my own mother. Without a doubt, my interest in religion and the Christian faith was due much more to her than to any school I ever attended. She was my main Bible teacher.

As I've already mentioned, she knew all the Gospel readings by heart as a result of her regular, attentive participation in worship services. She used to call me to sit with her after the vesper services in the evening so that she could tell me in her own words the meaning of the Gospel that would be read the next day. Her religion was alive; it was in no way theoretical.

Partly as a consequence of my own experience, I believe that whenever possible a person's first Bible teacher should be what I call a "practicing parent"—a father or mother who really believes and lives the faith. The practicing parent reads the Bible regularly to her youngsters and explains what those words mean in everyday life. As a result, the child receives profound lessons about faith that will stay with him in some form throughout his life.

I can remember visiting President Dwight Eisenhower in his Oval Office about thirty years ago on my return from a trip to Geneva. He told me that one of his most important early memories was listening to his father tell Bible stories to the children in his family. The older man would use a Greek text and translate the words into English as he spoke. At the time, although Eisenhower was only about eight or nine years old, he began to learn some of the basics of Scripture. And he said this early religious teaching influenced him in some fashion throughout his life.

Unfortunately, parents today don't emphasize Bible teaching at home in the same way that mothers and fathers did in the past. As I've pondered why things have changed so much, several thoughts have come to mind. For one thing, past generations of parents may have had more time to teach and educate their children in spiritual matters because life was less hectic. There were fewer things to compete for one's time at home, such as television.

Also, parents of past generations undoubtedly knew more about the Bible and were more committed to communicate their religious faith than most parents today. As our culture has become more secularized, Bible knowledge and teaching seem to have declined abruptly—especially after the generation that entered adulthood in the 1960s. This sixties generation of adults apparently have failed to pass on whatever they know about the Bible to their children. As a result, we now find ourselves confronted with a new generation that knows little or nothing about the stories, principles, and precepts of the Old and New Testaments.

Of course, sometimes the lessons that children are taught at a tender age by parents don't "take" in the sense of becoming a part of that child's life for all time. Eventually, when the child grows up, he must decide for himself whether he really believes what he has been taught about God's love, faith, and personal and social morality.

But if a mother or father really *loves* the child and reads and teaches the Bible to the youngster in a compassionate, understanding atmosphere, the chances are excellent that this early teaching will be the first step in a lifelong walk of faith.

At least, that was true in my own case, and it's also been true with many other serious Christians I've known.

So it's helpful to get a head start with Bible study as a child under the tutelage of a "practicing parent." Then, as an adult, it's essential to continue to learn Scriptural truth through a teacher who is also immersed in living the Christian life.

To put this another way, the Bible does not contain just "head knowledge," which is to be intellectually absorbed and memorized. Certainly, there is a factual foundation to Scripture that we should all have to one degree or another. But the facts without the Spirit will never change a life.

In a similar vein, St. Paul refers to the Word of God as the "sword of the Spirit," a term which implies strong, solid substance as well as a responsive, God-based source of inspiration and power. The sword without the spirit is a dead weapon. Yet the Spirit without the sword lacks the cutting edge of concrete authority.

So Bible study is an essential ingredient in any experience of spiritual growth, and that study must be done under the guidance of another, more experienced Christian—a student of the Scriptures who can communicate his own faith to you, even as he teaches factual and theological materials. Your teacher *must* be a believer. With any other type of teacher, you'll be using your head but not your heart.

Actually, I'd much rather sit in on a good Bible study than listen to the most inspiring sermon. For that matter, I'd rather *teach* a Bible study to a congregation than deliver a sermon. Many times, the inspiring sermon will impress you for the moment, but then you'll forget about it. A well-prepared Bible study, on the other hand, can remain with you for a much longer period of time—and sometimes even for life.

I've mentioned before that, when I'm participating in a worship experience, the words of the liturgy often seem quite fresh to me, even if I've heard them many, many times in the past. The reason for this is that God's Spirit can use the same words in a variety of different ways at different times in our lives.

The same principle applies to Scripture study. When I hear a Bible lesson on a particular passage, or when I ponder a particular text in the quiet of my study, God may show me one thing on one day. But then he may reveal something quite different on another occasion. This living quality of Scripture is one of the surest signs of divine inspiration—a "breathing" of God's vitality into the text from the moment the words were written nearly two millennia ago.

As we delve into the Bible for guidance and truth, we are participating in a centuries-old practice that goes back to the very foundation of the church. Just after Peter delivered his magnificent sermon after the first Pentecost, 3,000 new believers decided to follow Christ. What specific steps did they take? Luke tells us in Acts 2:42 that they began to develop their relationship with the Savior through the prayers, through the breaking of the bread or Holy Communion, through interactions with other believers—*and* through the Apostles' teaching. Today, the teaching of the Apostles comes to us through what they wrote in the Bible.

In this same spirit, it's my dream that increasing numbers of lay people will gather at the feet of qualified and believing teachers and learn the basics of spirituality that the Bible offers. At the same time, I'd like to see those same lay people get so excited about what they're hearing that they spend increasing amounts of time alone, exploring the deep well of Scripture and drawing forth its living waters.

With such an approach to the Bible, Christians will inevitably move forward in the faith. Most important of all, they'll be encouraged to keep their eyes constantly focused on Jesus, about whom the Scriptures speak and toward whom they have always pointed.

10

The Cross

For me, the cross is the ultimate symbol of hope.

One reason for my hope is that the cross often contravenes ordinary human expectations and understandings. Take the thief on the cross. He had little time to repent, to catalogue his past sins and renounce them one by one. He had no time to be baptised. He had no time to do good works, to develop spiritual disciplines like prayer, or to make any kind of contribution to a Christian movement.

The thief just said to his fellow robber, "This man has done nothing wrong." And then he asked, "Jesus, remember me when you come into your kingdom."

And Jesus replied, "Truly, I say to you, today you will be with me in Paradise."

This thief, the most intimate human companion of Jesus during those moments when both hung dying, reminds us that the cross of Christ is a disconcerting, disturbing, and life-giving focus for our faith. When I contemplate the cross, I become intensely aware of my own sinfulness. I feel profoundly sorry for my inability to correct the sins, actions, and thoughts that separate me from God and from other men and women.

Yet as I look more closely at the cross, I see a man hanging on it who understood everything about human nature. He knew all the weaknesses of men and women, for he had experienced personally the great challenges and temptations that we face every day. As a result, he has great compassion for us.

Without this experience of having been limited in the flesh, I question whether Christ ever could have asked his Father to pardon or forgive those who were crucifying him. Also, I wonder if Jesus, without understanding our foibles and flaws so intimately, would have decided freely to be raised up in spiritual and physical agony, in the full view and ridicule of his persecutors.

After all, he did have a choice. We know that. Yet in the Garden of Gethsemane he chose to die for us, for you and for me. Only a man with the most intimate understanding and experience of the human condition could have made such a self-sacrificing decision. As the Son of God he was in the form of God, St. Paul tells us. Yet he chose to empty himself, take on the form of a servant, and even be crucified for the sake of those who would follow him.

Jesus' submission to death on the cross was the perfect expression of human love. Again, I return to the example of the child. A loving parent will always put the welfare of his child ahead of himself. If a child needs help with his basic welfare, his education—even his music lessons or athletic equipment—the devoted parent will sacrifice to fulfill his youngster's needs.

For that matter, most parents would give their own lives

if that meant their child could be saved and freed to follow in the parents' footsteps. In a sense, that's what Jesus did for us. He sacrificed himself for your benefit and mine, so that we could follow in his divine footsteps.

Yet, in many ways his sacrifice on the cross remains disconcerting and disturbing. For one thing, contrary to human assumptions about the importance of seniority, he doesn't care how recently we have come into his family. Also, contrary to our heavy emphasis on personal achievement and success, he doesn't expect us to become perfect—or even get close to perfection. He died even for those who are the last to arrive and who are in the worst sort of shape. He accepts us at any time, in any condition, just so long as we believe in him and rely on him, as did the thief on the cross.

In some ways, I think that the Pascal Oration of St. John Chrysostom puts it better than any other passage in the classic liturgy. During the reading of St. John's oration, many people experience the resurrection itself, as they shout in the early morning hours of Easter Day, "He is risen!"

Now, listen and ponder some of these words of St. John Chrysostom, which have a direct bearing on the cross:

"He that had arrived only at the eleventh hour, let him not be afraid by reason of his delay. The Lord is gracious and receives the last as the first. He giveth rest to him that cometh the eleventh hour, as well as him that has toiled from the first.

"Ye first and last receive alike the reward. Ye rich and poor rejoice together. Ye sober and ye slothful celebrate. He that has kept the fast and he that has not, rejoice, for the table is richly laden.

"Let no one mourn that he has fallen again and again, for he has risen from the grave. Let no one fear death, for the

death of our Savior has set us free. He has destroyed death by
enduring it. . . .

"Oh death where is thy sting? Oh Hades where thy vic-
tory? Christ is risen! [The people shout, 'Christ is risen!'] . . .
Christ is risen and the evil ones are cast down. Christ is risen
and the angels rejoice. Christ is risen and life is liberated.
Christ is risen and the tomb is empty of the dead. . . . To
him be glory and power forever and ever."

These words reflect a belief that can open the heavens for
you. It's a belief that sees no classes among people, which
invites all to a new life, a life that cannot be measured by days
or years, but by joy and faith and hope. This is what St. John
Chrysostom believes about the cross and about God's forgiv-
ing love—and it's what I believe as well.

11

Memory and Imagination

The most precious gift of God to man is memory. Memory sustains me much of the time when I'm in spiritual turmoil, when I'm in the grip of doubt, confusion, or hesitancy.

Often, my most important memories concern things I learned as a child, or recollections of principles I was taught by people in my village who had lived long, virtuous lives. Sometimes, too, I may recall something my mother told me decades ago, or an event I witnessed in my village that carried some important, enduring message.

When I need a sustaining memory in the present, God's Spirit always seems to respond in calling up the past event or lesson to consciousness. And more often than not, what comes to my mind, along with that particular past event or lesson, will be a passage of Scripture.

There is a strong emphasis throughout the Bible on the importance of memorizing spiritual principles and Scriptural passages. The Psalmist says in Psalm 119:11, "Thy word have I hid in mine heart, that I might not sin against thee." When the inspired words of God in Scripture are indelibly imprinted on our minds, we possess a reservoir of constructive information, principles, and guidance that God can use at any time to correct, comfort, or inspire.

Sometimes, I'll think, "I'm not giving my life as completely to God as I should be doing. I'm becoming too entangled in the cares of the world, in administration, and management. I'm not being attentive enough to cultivating my relationship with God in prayer and meditation."

When I get in such moods, it's easy to berate myself, to think that in a spiritual sense I'm going backward, rather than forward. Even though I know what I should be doing and what I want to do, I simply can't seem to do it!

At such times, God often brings to mind one of my favorite passages of Scripture, the seventh chapter of St. Paul's letter to the Romans. There, I see Paul experiencing exactly what I myself am feeling. He says, "I can will what is right, but I cannot do it. For I do not do the good I want, but the evil I do not want is what I do."

Yet even as Paul cries out with me in anguish, in that same passage he also gives me an answer: "Who will deliver me from this body of death? Thanks be to God through Jesus Christ our Lord!"

Perhaps you can begin to see now why I feel that the memory is the greatest and most precious gift that God has given us. When I recall words like those Paul wrote in Romans 7, I no longer feel alone in my struggles. I know that one of the greatest followers of Jesus also experienced some of the same emotions and the sense of failure that I sometimes feel. At the same time, my memory of this passage of Scripture gives me cause for hope, just as Paul indicated that he drew hope from Jesus Christ his Lord.

So memory isn't by any means limited to abstract or dead recollections of the past. Rather, my memory has a direct bearing on the way I feel and function right now, in the tumultuous present.

Also, memory of the past combines with present imagination to create a more exciting and focused future. I find, when I think deeply about it, that I can't really separate memory from imagination. They're on a kind of continuum in my mind. I remember important events and facts, words of principle and promise, from the liturgy and from Scripture. These thoughts flow from my past into the present and they trigger ideas and visions that help me plan for the future.

As human beings, our ability to remember important things and then use those memories in our imaginations enables us to live simultaneously in the past, the present and the future. To my mind, these two very rich elements in our nature, memory and imagination, are major factors that distinguish us, as reasonable, self-conscious beings, from animals.

Also, you might say that our memories help to make our faith "portable." Typically, we may spend designated times by ourselves or in the company of other believers studying, praying, and worshiping. At those times, our spirits are being nourished through spiritual disciplines. But still, those disciplines are, in a sense, tied down to certain times and places.

Most of our daily lives, on the other hand, are spent on the move. We're constantly traveling, commuting, attending meetings, writing reports, or interacting in various ways with others. In such mobile circumstances, we have no time or opportunity to pursue the more static practices of Bible study, group prayer, or quiet, solitary meditation.

But in such chaotic, fast-moving circumstances, memory saves us. If we have filled our minds with the Scriptures and with past lessons from other believers, we can draw on those memories no matter where we are and no matter how many pressures we face. If the memories are there, God will bring them to mind to support us, comfort us, and nourish our spirits. I know he will do this because I've experienced his gift of memory on many occasions, as I deal daily with my own high-pressured, on-the-move existence.

In short, memory can provide a freedom of the spirit, a constant source of inspiration and divine nurturance, that would otherwise be impossible. One of our major goals, then, should be to cultivate those memories that can give us the most help and support as we move along the lifetime path of faith.

To this end, we should expose ourselves to those people and situations that will build us up, rather than tear us down. We should truly *remember* Jesus, as he commanded us to do, when we partake of Holy Communion. We should "hide in our hearts," through study and memorization, those words of Scripture and those experiences of the spiritual life that God can use to help us and guide us through life's many challenges.

With such preparation, our memories and imaginations will be combined in new and more creative ways. And we'll be provided with a new liberation of our spirits and a more exuberant awareness of the salvation of our souls.

12

The True Test
of Time

We live in a time-obsessed society.

The upwardly mobile and achievement-oriented among us are always trying to do things more quickly and more efficiently. Yet, while the pace of our lives accelerates, we don't usually enjoy greater inner peace or personal satisfaction. Instead, the pressures on us increase as we try to maintain a high level of quality in our activities. In effect, we seem to want to live two or three complete lives in the space of one!

As our lives move ahead faster and faster, sometimes at near-blinding speeds, to what end are we heading? Usually, even when we take time to think about it, our goals are limited to getting more money, elevating our personal or professional status, or eliciting the praise and approval of some respected superior or peer group.

In any event, the accelerated pace certainly doesn't make life happier or more meaningful. Instead, we become more regimented and constricted. We have few cushions of free time that we can use to unwind, decompress, and, most important of all, get to know God. It often takes intelligent, ambitious, well-meaning human beings a substantial part of a lifetime to realize a simple, self-evident fact: Time is not something that human beings, operating by themselves, can tame, expand, or shorten.

Too often, we make the mistake of assuming that time is just a succession of events, which by our own manipulations we can streamline and organize to perfection. We believe it's entirely within our power to "make the best use of our time."

Such reductionistic, time-management thinking causes us to measure our lives with our watches or with time-punch machines in factories and offices. Even intelligent managers assume, quite erroneously, that if they have a certain number of warm human bodies present in an office for a certain number of hours a day, they are likely to get a great deal more accomplished. In short, they'll be more successful if they can just keep a close watch on their subordinates' time.

But in fact, truly creative work cannot be measured in this way. Many times, people must rely on their personal judgment to make decisions, or they may be assigned a project that requires some imagination and thought. In such cases, they can't quantify their effective daily working time in terms of six, seven, or eight hours.

Of course, most projects and assignments do require a minimum number of hours to accomplish. You can't write a high-quality book or establish a successful new business in a day or a week. Many more days and weeks are necessary to give the "creative juices" an opportunity to flow and to produce a final result that will satisfy. But still, work that is excellent and creative can't really be evaluated in terms of how much time you've put in: The essential standard for measuring success is the result you achieve, regardless of how much time you have spent in completing the job.

As Christians, we have been handed the gift of time for one major purpose: To create new things in our lives for God. Yet too often, like everyone else in our secularized culture, we don't see time as an opportunity for creation. Rather, we see it as something to be measured mechanistically or used up by a clock.

But from God's perspective, time is never self-limiting, never measured entirely by minutes, hours, and days. Instead, time always has an eternal dimension. St. John underlines this fact when he says in the first verse of his Gospel, "In the beginning was the Word. . . ." Those are frightening words because they emphasize to us our limited natures in the face of God's limitless reality.

Who, after all, can locate "the beginning"? Yet as human beings, we're always trying to understand, define, and control our time. In our own little worlds, we try to be gods who know exactly when something is going to happen, when it will begin, and when it will end. But when we fall into this trap, we become the slaves rather than the masters of time.

Too often, we fail to put God in charge of our daily schedules and our various responsibilities, so that he can show us how best to use creatively the time he's given us. We may devote many minutes and sometimes hours to setting up our schedules and filling in our daily appointment diaries. For a time, we may even seem to get things organized in this way. But in fact, more often than not, we lose our creative edge in the process.

The insidious thing about this obsessive approach to time management is that comprehensive scheduling can give you a false sense of accomplishment. Certainly, it does make you feel as though you've made some progress when you can check off several items on your daily list of "things to do." But even if you've finished three or four things today, what has been the quality of your work? How much satisfaction have you derived from what you've done? Have you been creative or an idle thinker in dealing with your daily tasks?

Like any busy person, I have a daily schedule that I follow. I attend meetings that are set by appointment, and I think it's very important to be on time for these meetings and limit their duration. Otherwise, we'll waste and violate the time of others.

But once I've met the obligations and attended the meetings that I know are necessary, I like to set aside some open-ended periods when I can be creative and free of the constraints of scheduling.

For example, I never measure the time I spend at work. I'll think, write, and make decisions as the Spirit moves me, but I'll try to avoid situations where I'm likely to feel that I have to complete my work at a certain precise time. Rather, I prefer to stop work when I feel that I cannot continue productively. For my work hours to be creative, my focus must be on the task at hand, on the objectives I want to accomplish, and on the presence of God in the process of work. If I'm always looking at the clock, I limit myself. More importantly, I limit God and I limit the possibility for true creativity. As a result, the quality of my work will decrease significantly.

Too often, it seems to me, emphasizing that a job must be completed precisely within a certain time frame can destroy rather than enhance the quality of the work that is produced. The concepts of "overtime" and punching the time clock are inventions of people who are more interested in mechanical work than in achieving excellence. Of course, you don't have to have a physical time clock or be subject to rules of overtime to fall into this fallacy. I know many executives who keep such precise track of their daily schedules that they have in effect created their *own* time clocks! They can tell you hour by hour, and frequently minute by minute, exactly what they were doing on a given day.

Certainly, writing down appointments in a daily diary and setting up a daily schedule can be helpful. In fact, it's probably essential to have events and duties written down somewhere so that you don't miss appointments or arrive for them late. But an overemphasis on such scheduling can negate our true humanity and bring us to a state of being instruments of time, rather than children of God.

So at one extreme, overscheduling our lives reflects an effort on our part to "play God" over our daily schedules, a role for which imperfect human beings are certainly ill-fitted. At the other extreme, though, some people ignore time completely. As a result, they fail to see the eternal dimension that is present in our daily lives.

I can recall one woman who was given responsibility to teach a Sunday school class. She spent some time preparing her lesson based on a particular Bible text. Then, she brought the written materials she needed to class to get the important points across to the children.

Unfortunately, though, her sense of the eternal priorities of her mission weren't too clear. In the first few minutes, she noticed that the children in her class seemed much more interested in doing fingerpainting and spending extra time with their refreshments than they were in the Bible lesson. So this teacher didn't assert herself and urge the students toward more productive activities. Instead, she just let them do as they pleased. As a result, they left that morning not knowing a bit more about the Bible than when they had come in.

Obviously, this woman had no understanding of how the eternal God could use her, as a temporal being, in communicating a message of divine truth and love to these youngsters. In effect, by not discovering God's presence in the temporal world, she wasted her time—and also the time of her young charges.

Our time, then, is not a mere succession of events. It's not a series of projects and responsibilities that we are supposed to compress and streamline according to some human preconceptions. Nor is time a vacuum to be filled by any sort of whimsical activity. Rather, time is God's gift to us. It is he—not others or ourselves—who has the authority to determine how the minutes and hours of our lives can be best used.

If we allow others to dictate the way our time will be used, or if we try to assume complete control over the schedule ourselves, we're sure to face frustration and failure. But if we allow God to help us "redeem the time," as St. Paul puts it in his letter to the Colossians, we'll find ourselves becoming more creative. We'll also experience greater satisfaction as we move through our daily tasks; and we'll find the quality of our work improving.

In short, we must become more aware of God's eternal presence in every hour and minute of each day. That's the true test of time in our lives.

13

The Divine Light

A lifetime of faith is also a lifetime filled with light.

Whenever God is present with us, his divine light is there as well. Yet this light is not the same as the light of a lightbulb or even the light of the sun. Certainly, God's light involves a shining or radiance, which may remind us of the ordinary lights we encounter in our lives each day. But the divine light also involves much more.

God's light is his glory, or *doxa,* which emanates from his very presence. The result is not just a brightening up of things so that we can read better or see each other more clearly. Rather, the beams of his personal glory radiate throughout our spirits and have the power to warm our souls and change our lives.

God's light has shone on mankind in a variety of powerful and sometimes disturbing ways throughout history. Moses, who had been in God's presence for many days on Mount

Sinai, came back down with his face shining. The reflection of God's glory was so powerful in him that he had to wear a veil over his face to avoid frightening his fellow Israelites. The shepherds were filled with this fear when the glory of God radiated about them as the angels announced the birth of Christ. And St. Paul, when he encountered Christ on the Road to Damascus, was knocked to the ground and blinded with the divine light of the Savior.

Obviously, then, God's light carries tremendous power as well as physical brightness. In fact, the hidden, inner power of the divine light may sometimes quite literally "outshine" any physical brilliance. I've been especially impressed with the dynamic force of this inner light when I've visited some of the historic sites in the Holy Land.

On my first visit to Bethlehem, I was in the company of several of the world's leading Christian clergymen, including the then Secretary of the World Council of Churches, another top official of the World Council, and the dean of a leading Lutheran seminary. Together, we walked down into the grotto that is the traditional site of the stable where Jesus was born and placed in a manger.

These men were administrators and practical managers, who seemed unlikely to be emotionally or spiritually moved by a trip to a religious tourist site. But as we entered the actual grotto and stood before the candles that had been lit around the traditional location of the manger, we experienced a mighty spiritual moment. These men, who I had been thinking were primarily hard-headed, secular-oriented realists, fell to their knees before I did! And the very man whom I had regarded as the *most* secular of the lot began to cry uncontrollably.

What had happened here? I can only say that there is a

power of God's presence that may break through at unexpected times and in unexpected places in our lives. In this particular case, we were literally *forced* to kneel by a kind of divine weight, as we worshiped before an empty manger, a manger where two thousand years before the light of Christ had come into the world.

I can't analyze such a moment. I don't even feel the need to seek a rational understanding of it. You can only *live* times like these, and the more intensely you live them, the better your life will be.

Even today, as I think about that moment or try to talk about it, I can hardly hold back my tears. I can hardly speak without having my voice shake. On that occasion, God's divine light broke through in a special way to enhance my life and the lives of those churchmen who were with me. The only physical light that I saw was those quiet candles, burning and glowing around the rocks and steps in that cave inside the church. But the light I *felt* was a beam of warmth, comfort, and inspiration that radiated throughout my whole being and linked me in some inexplicable, mystical way to my companions.

Experiences like these constitute a fleeting, but foundation-shaking, encounter with the light that illuminated Jesus at his Transfiguration . . . the light Ezekiel saw glowing in God's temple . . . the light that illumined the robes of the angels who guarded the empty tomb. Most important of all, such experiences enable us to understand in a more personal way the words of Jesus, who said in St. John's Gospel, "I am the light of the world; he who follows me will not walk in darkness, but will have the light of life."

14

The Peace That
Passes Understanding

We live in what has been called the Age of Anxiety. We agonize over the past; we are nervous about the present; and we worry incessantly about the future.

Material possessions don't remedy the problem because our anxieties run rampant in the midst of unprecedented affluence. The more money and goods we have, the more things we have to worry about. Our advanced medical and technological knowledge doesn't help much either. The pills, prescriptions, and labor-saving devices we've invented either pave the way to addictions or a multitude of other worries and problems we never faced before.

Of course, we're by no means the first people to experience overwhelming waves of worries in our daily lives. Those living under the ancient Roman Empire also lived in an "Age of Anxiety," and the first Christians were as vulnerable to the worries and cares of their daily lives as we are today.

Jesus recognized this serious emotional challenge on a number of occasions, and he encouraged his followers to confront the problem and deal with it. In the Sermon on the Mount, for example, he said, "Therefore do not be anxious about tomorrow, for tomorrow will be anxious for itself. Let the day's own trouble be sufficient for the day."

Yet how, exactly, do we get rid of our anxieties? Is there some practical approach we can use to deal with these daily worries and concerns, which often make life miserable?

St. Paul pointed the way to an answer in one of the most helpful passages in his epistles, Philippians 4:6–7:

> Have no anxiety about anything, but in everything by prayer and supplication with thanksgiving let your requests be made known to God. And the peace of God, which passes all understanding, will keep your hearts and your minds in Christ Jesus. (RSV)

This is a passage of Scripture worth studying and meditating upon in your daily devotions. You might go off by yourself and spend fifteen minutes, a half hour, even an hour or more focusing on these words. Ponder over and over this powerful, compressed pair of sentences, which contain much of what we need to deal with the anxieties of our lives.

In this passage, Paul, like Jesus, begins with a command: Stop having anxiety! The solution begins with an act of the will. If anxiety comes upon you, you needn't expect some magical solution to your problem. The solution lies within yourself and your relationship with Christ.

So what can you do? Paul says first that you should offer prayers of supplication *with thanksgiving*. In other words, in an honest, conversational way, tell God how you feel about what's bothering you. Yet even as you tell him, thank him for all he means to you and for what you know he is doing to relieve your anxiety, even as you pray. By thanking God as you pray, you're demonstrating to him that you have faith in his power to act in your life.

Finally, as a result of prayers offered in faith, Paul says that you'll receive "the peace of God, which passes all understanding." And that peace will enable you to rest, without anxiety, in union with Christ.

But it's not necessary to quantify or reduce this peace to its component parts in order to enjoy its benefits. The peace of God is a divine and mysterious tranquillity that comes over us when we respond to him in obedience and give him control over our worries and anxieties. St. Peter says much the same thing as St. Paul, but in a somewhat different way, in his First Epistle: "Cast all your anxieties on him, for he cares about you." Again, we're commanded to take action—to get rid of those cares and worries that are plaguing us. Yet we don't just resort to the nearest available self-help strategy; we give them, in prayer, to Christ. And when we release them to him, he grants us his miraculous peace, which transcends human understanding.

The Greek word for the peace that Paul and others talk about is *eirene*, a term that implies an experience of harmony, or an interlocking of separate parts. Take your hands and clasp them together, with the fingers intertwined around one another. This interlocking of your hands and fingers is a physical symbol of the *eirene*, or peace, which the Scriptures tell us about.

The reason that this kind of peace is so difficult, if not impossible, to understand is that it involves a full integration of all our faculties so that we experience inner harmony. Our hearts and minds interlock around one single set of priorities, which center on our decision to place all our cares, worries, and anxieties into the hands of Christ. In a very real sense, this kind of peace involves becoming one with God in Christ. The peace of God that surpasses human understanding is a peace that involves unity with God.

Also, just as true inner peace is possible only when we're united with God, peace among peoples or nations is possible only when there is a kind of spiritual unity and integration. Unfortunately, however, I've seen this kind of peace occur between people only in limited circumstances and for relatively short periods of time. For example, I've seen people in prayer groups reach a reasonable facsimile of this kind of unity as they open themselves up to one another and pray about mutual concerns. God's peace descends upon them when jointly, as a group, they let their requests be made known in prayer and cast their anxieties on him.

But as I say, instances of this kind of group peace seem to occur infrequently and in limited circumstances. More often, when we have meetings involving various interest groups in our society—or among nations or even religious denominations—the agreements reached through negotiation and compromise don't constitute true peace or unity. Rather, they just amount to a truce. There's an absence of war until the next misunderstanding or conflict occurs.

As you can see, I'm not too optimistic about the achievement of lasting peace between large groups of people. I've seen peace talks of various types fail too often in my life to hold out much hope for this sort of thing in the future. Too often, when we're seeking peace, we don't look for it on God's terms. Rather, we pursue peace out of human self-interest. That sort of motivation may lead to some temporary settlements, but not to lasting spiritual unity. The peace of God, which St. Paul and others talk about in the New Testament is truly a different phenomenon.

But I'm more optimistic about the development of peace inside individuals and within small groups of committed believers. When a genuine allegiance to Christ is present and there's a willingness to put him in charge of the cares and anxieties that are bothering us, true peace becomes a very real possibility.

As I ponder the words of Scripture on peace and anxiety and try to make them my own, I find that often I achieve peace when I follow three main steps:

Step #1: I individualize my expectations of peace.

I focus first on the fact that true peace must begin within me, not on the outside in some sort of general peace negotiations or meetings. I can't expect my inner peace to be imposed from without, by other human beings. I may learn something about peace from the spiritual journeys of other believers. But ultimately, the peace that I can experience has to be something between me and God.

To put this another way, the peace that passes understanding must always arise out of a deep relationship with Christ. If there is no such relationship, there's no possibility of God-given inner tranquillity and integration.

Step #2: I identify the source of my anxieties.

First, I'll ask myself a simple direct question: "What is my anxiety?"

At the essence of most anxiety is dislocation—an "out-of-jointness" that separates me from others and God. Usually, when I'm anxious, I find that I've allowed myself to trust more in my own powers and priorities than in those available to me through my faith.

At one time, when I was considerably younger, I had the ambition to be noticed by others, to be recognized and respected for my accomplishments. If I sensed that there was some possibility that I might not be recognized or looked up to sufficiently, that could make me anxious.

Others become anxious about material things. I've known many men and women who spent most of their intellectual abilities and their time trying to accumulate as much wealth as possible. Yet inevitably people who are concerned about such things are never satisfied. They frequently become worried about how much they can increase their status or income, or how their investments will fare in an uncertain stock or bond market. They become anxious because to one degree or another, they are separated from the ultimate source of peace and proper priorities; they are separated from God.

Certainly, I've experienced common worldly anxieties, as has every other human being. Yet I'm always happy when I can identify the source of my anxiety. Then, I know I've taken a major step toward overcoming that anxiety and finding God's peace.

Too often, we avoid taking a close *second* look at our true selves and the actual priorities we've set for our lives. We become so busy or insensitive to the motives that are driving us that we in effect allow blindfolds to cover the eyes of our hearts. We can't see what it is that's making us dislocated from our true selves, what's preventing us from finding complete inner integration as God's children.

So it's extremely important for the Christian to have the ability to take a second look at himself. It's essential for him to see exactly what his priorities are and what interests he's serving.

Step #3: I agonize for God's peace.

As we've seen, St. Paul says that we should stop having anxiety and pray with thanksgiving that God will help us get rid of our worries and experience true peace. But this type of prayer does not come easily. It takes work—hard, agonizing work. We must meet God in an intense, private encounter that may last for many minutes or even hours. We must agonize in his presence, waiting for him to respond and show us the direction we should take to find relief from our anxieties.

In a sense, we're confronted here with a paradox. We must agonize in order to break free from agony. Yet this kind of agony-to-banish-agony doesn't lead to the human anxieties that cause inner dislocation and worry. Rather, this is a kind of *holy* agony that makes us uncomfortable until we find God's will for our lives.

Jesus experienced this holy agony in the Garden of Gethsemane just before his crucifixion, as he sought to conform his will to the Father's. Also, I suspect that he went through a similar kind of holy agony as he spent all night in prayer before choosing the twelve disciples.

I no longer experience the concern and anxiety that may have arisen from my ambition to be noticed when I was younger. But today, I get anxious about other things. I get worried and even frightened when I think of the gifts and blessings that I have received from God—and my very inadequate response to him in using these gifts. So now, I find that I must agonize in prayer in an effort to find his will for my life, including how my gifts can best be used.

As a result, my anxieties today focus mostly on how I can

live my life in a more Christian way. Also, I want to leave behind a more godly community after I die. I want the rich and the poor in our Christian communities, the well-educated and the illiterate, to focus not on the concerns of this world, but rather on the concerns of God. I want them to be illuminated by the light of the Holy Spirit—and I worry whether I'm doing enough to achieve this end. This is my present anxiety, something I constantly agonize over in my prayers.

I wouldn't want to give the impression that in the midst of all this anxiety and agonizing, I experience little of God's peace. In fact, as the years have gone by, I've found that the "peace that passes understanding" regularly becomes much more a part of my life. Still, I find that there's an ongoing dynamic, or spiritual pendulum swing, between the anxieties that I feel and the peace that God gives me to relieve those anxieties.

So the anxiety is still there in my life, but the spiritual tools which God has given me to deal with it are more powerful. I only pray that he will continue to draw me into a more perfect union with him. And I trust that day by day, he will teach me more about this wonderful peace, which will always remain just outside the reach of my human understanding.

15

Casting Out Fear

Many people live in a constant state of fear. They are afraid that some "ax" is going to fall on them, even if they're not quite sure they've done anything wrong.

People I meet every day quake before a multitude of possibilities. They fear that they'll lose their job . . . that they'll fail to achieve some personal or professional goal . . . that they'll be lonely for the rest of their lives . . . that they or a loved one may fall victim to a dread disease . . . that they or a loved one will die an untimely death.

In short, just as we live in an Age of Anxiety, we also live in an Age of Fear. But what exactly *is* fear? In a sense, fear and anxiety are really part of the same package. They're part of an intensifying stream of emotions that begin with slight worry; move through deeper and deeper anxiety; and finally culminate in the sheer, raw terror of our worst nightmares.

On another, more fundamental level, fear is the terror or

dread that comes upon a person when he feels that he may be on the verge of losing any connection with God—that he may be on the very brink of total extinction. Anxieties may start us off in this direction, but they can only hint at the excruciating spiritual and emotional pain of raw fear.

To put this in another way, fear arises from the absence of God's love in a person's life. Of course, God's love is always available to anyone who wishes to receive it. But many times, we ignore the hand that God lovingly holds out to comfort, encourage, and guide us into his family circle. When we neglect or turn away from his love, worries, anxieties, and finally deep fears may grab hold of us.

Yet, when we open ourselves to God's love and let his compassion and concern for us fill our lives, fear fades and eventually disappears. As St. John puts it in his First Epistle, "There is no fear in love; but perfect love casts out fear. . . ."

Why does a lack of love cause us to be fearful? St. John goes on to explain that fear is linked to punishment, while God's love through the sacrifice of his Son has removed the threat of ultimate punishment. Yet many times, we allow the power of God's love to slip away from us, and the dread of punishment to creep back in.

Sometimes, this happens because we disobey God in some way and, as a result, we develop a guilty conscience. There's a very deep sense within us that if we violate God's laws or step outside his will, something bad may happen. Some punishment may strike.

Some might argue that such feelings of guilt are unhealthy, and we should do everything in our power, through psychotherapy or any other means, to get rid of them. But I'm not so sure. I think that feelings of guilt, those prickings of a conscience that has been violated by certain improper or immoral acts, may be a very healthy thing. After all, the rules of behavior that God has established in this world are not optional. The universe operates according to certain laws relating to our health, our sexuality, our personal morality, and our relationships. And there are likely to be consequences if we decide we won't follow those laws.

Still, I'm not one of those people who believes that God will routinely reach down from some seat in heaven and smack us if we step out of line. The way he operates is generally much more loving, subtle, and parental than that. More often, when we step outside God's will and begin trying to live by our own wills, we'll get a sense that something is not quite right. Often, we may first experience anxiety; then, a wave of fear may sweep over us, as we wonder where our lives are going and what traps we may fall into.

There are good grounds for these feelings of concern and fear. For example, if we begin to violate God's will for our sexuality, we'll not only experience emotional misgivings; we may also put our health at serious risk. In fact, the fears that we feel from a guilty conscience after we stray from God's will for our lives may provide important signals that our very existence as spiritual beings is in jeopardy.

But sometimes, serious fears can arise when our consciences are relatively clear. Often, the reason for this fear is that we lack sufficient faith or depth in our relationship with God. A classic case of this kind of fear might occur on a battlefield.

When one young man was serving in a particular military service under combat conditions, he enjoyed the excitement of battle. But then, as the weeks and months passed, he began to realize that war was not really much fun. In fact, he might even be killed.

During one particularly devastating rocket attack, while he was lying prostrate on the ground with explosions going off around him, he was gripped by a feeling of raw terror. He began to ask himself: "What am I doing here? I'm barely twenty-five years old. I have a young wife at home, and I may never get out of this place alive. I have everything to live for, and yet my life may be cut off in the next instant!"

Although this young man believed in God, he suddenly realized that his faith was not quite what he wanted it to be. He also recalled that his decision to participate in this particular war had been his and his alone. God had had very little to do with his choice. This fellow had been following *his* will for his life, rather than God's. Now, it looked as though he might not be around much longer to find out what God wanted for him in the future.

In fact, the young man did survive, and he finally returned home, where he resumed his relationship with his wife, raised a family, and pursued a rewarding career. But still, he knew the fear that he had felt—the terror of total extinction, of being eternally outside of God's will—had been very real. So he began to seek God's guidance for his life during ensuing years. As he continued his spiritual journey, he frequently looked back to his combat experiences as a major milestone that had helped direct him toward a more serious Christian commitment.

Even those who are more deeply involved in a relationship with Christ may occasionally find themselves beset by fears that go far beyond ordinary anxiety. For example, one father with a small, elementary-school child experienced a series of confidence-shaking fears that something terrible might happen to his son. He had no particular reason to think that a tragedy might occur. But sometimes, his imagination would begin to run wild. In a compulsive, destructive daydream he might picture his child being abducted or run over by a car on the street.

"What would I do if something like that happened?" he asked. "I'm really not sure I could go on living my life as I have in the past. I think I might be so upset that I'd never recover from such a thing."

Fortunately, this man finally realized that the fears he occasionally felt about his child arose from a lack of faith, a lack of development in his relationship with Christ. If he had really believed that God was in control of every aspect of his life—including his son's future—then he would have felt more secure and peaceful. He would have been able to pray, "God, I know you're in control of everything that happens to me and everything that happens to my son. So I'm just going to turn our lives over to you. I'm asking you to guide me and remove this sense of fear that I'm feeling."

In effect, this is what this man was finally able to do after he had spent some time praying and studying the Scriptures. He finally understood that love and fear are intimately connected in the Christian life. And he also saw that the power of love can banish fear.

This father eventually realized that a much healthier kind of fear he should be feeling was the fear of *God,* and not of possible tragedies that might occur. This fear of God is not a debilitating terror, but rather a deep, overwhelming sense of awe, reverence, and respect, a fear the Proverbs tell us is "the beginning of wisdom."

The fear of God and the love of God are closely linked throughout the Scriptures, from the Old Testament to the New. We are told to put ourselves completely in God's hands, trust him totally and without reservation. Then, when we acknowledge his power over our lives, we enter his presence with the sense of awe, reverence—and, yes, *fear*—that are appropriate attitudes for the children of the Creator of the universe.

So as we receive God's love, we can also expect to develop a healthy, constructive fear or awe about his power. Yet with an experience of God's love and a respect for his power, we'll find that the uncertainties and even the dangers of life hold no ordinary fears for us at all.

I've been very fortunate because since I was a young man, I've been free of the fear that arises from a dread of total extinction, the fear that's rooted in a sense of being separated from the love of God. Of course, when I was a child, I suffered many of the fears that plague young people. I worried about ghosts being around the corner of dark hallways, and I worried about unseen forces from which I was afraid my parents might not be able to protect me.

But after I began my walk with Christ, the anxieties I've felt about various issues have never turned into the raw kind of fear we've been discussing in the last few pages. The only explanation I can give for my lack of fear is a special grace or mercy that God must have felt I needed. In fact, without this protection from fear, I might have been immobilized by the many threats against my life.

I can recall on one occasion a number of years ago I was driven on various side roads through a roundabout route from downtown Detroit to the Detroit airport. As we went over a bridge, I saw policemen looking over it, and I suspected something serious was in the wind. But I didn't ask the people who were driving me because I just wasn't that worried about it.

Finally, when two policemen accompanied me onto my airplane, I asked one of them, "What's happened?"

"We got a telephone call that someone wanted to assassinate you on the way to the airport," I was told.

"Why? What have I done?"

"A group called and identified themselves as Turkish terrorists. They said that, because you're an enemy of Turkey, they've decided to kill you."

At the time, we had a demonstration going on in Washington for the rights of the Greeks in Cyprus, which was under Turkish rule.

Another time, after some meetings in New York in 1970, police joined me after I left an auditorium and hurried me toward my car.

"Why?" I asked again. "What's the reason? Why are you doing this?"

"We had a call that someone is hiding around here, waiting for the proper moment to kill you," they replied.

Sometimes, I think I should include such threats as a regular part of my schedule. When I was at a fundraising banquet for the Greek American high school in Jamaica, Queens, I began to greet people after the ceremonies were finished. But then six policemen surrounded me and began to lead me off toward the car. This time, I laughed and, as usual, I asked, "Why are you doing this?"

"We had several calls threatening to kill you," they answered.

Then, there was the time that I arrived in Greece, and eleven policemen surrounded my car on my arrival.

"Why this very official reception?" I asked them.

"We had a telephone call that someone was going to try to get you with a car bomb," they said.

I've confronted countless threats like this over the years. But curiously, I've never experienced fear. Of course, such threats don't make me happy, but my inner responses have nothing to do with my own safety. Rather, I feel sorry for people who are so full of hate that they feel they have to strike out physically at another person. I feel sorry for them because they lack a true relationship with God.

In all of these cases, I've had a very definite, even palpable sense of God's presence with me. Without the knowledge that God was there, I'm sure I would have been terrified. But with him next to me, there's no reason to fear. After all, if an assassin succeeds, what do I have to lose? Only my life. And if I die, that just means I will move on from this imperfect life to the perfect union with Christ.

As a matter of fact, I think that all feelings of raw fear or terror must arise in some way from a fear of death. The way that Christians deal with death is in many ways a fundamental, "bottom-line" factor in the way their faith develops. As we grow closer and closer to Christ in this life, the concern about death—that transition from this life to the next—should become less characterized by fear, and more by a sense of expectation and looking forward to the life of the spirit that is to come.

I know that St. Paul calls death the last enemy that we must face. But that enemy has already been defeated because Christ has overcome death through his resurrection. Certainly, I am concerned about my spiritual record in this life; I'm concerned about what God will say when I stand before him at the Last Judgment. I want him to say, "Well done," when he evaluates the way I've used the gifts he has given me. But in the last analysis, I'm not afraid of death because I trust in the mercy of God and in the saving act of his Son on the cross.

16

Death and Beyond

Occasionally, I'll imagine myself dead. In my mind's eye, I'll see my funeral ceremony taking place, with people passing by to pay their last respects.

I know that most, if not all, of them will be generous to me as my body is lying there before them. Yet, in a way, I find these daydreams funny. I see myself smiling up from my coffin at my well-wishers, thanking them for their generosity, but urging them gently to be a little more honest.

I'm well aware that it's not human judgments that count at such a moment, but rather the judgment of God. I can also almost hear God chuckling as he listens to the unqualified praises showered upon a person who was far from perfect.

I am completely confident that there's a life of the spirit that continues after this earthly life. But I must confess that I don't always have confidence about what my role will be in that next life. As I get older, I cling to the words of St. Paul in his First Epistle to the Thessalonians: "We shall always be with Christ." Yet I know that I am not St. Paul, and so I don't feel qualified to speak with his boldness and confidence.

But even as such questions occasionally come to my mind, God always seems to find a way to bolster my faith and let me know that he has a place for me in his eternal kingdom. About five years ago, for example, I was very sick in a hospital. A bishop was sitting beside me as I finished a light lunch that had been served at my bedside. But I had very little desire to eat. I could tell from the way the doctors and nurses had been bustling about me that I was not in very good shape, and the outlook for my recovery might not be too good.

Suddenly, however, as I pushed my food aside, I had a definite sense that my body was floating about two or three feet above the bed. I turned to the bishop and asked, "Look at my body. Am I floating over the bed, or am I lying on the bed?"

"You're on the bed," he said.

But still, I had that feeling that I was floating. In fact, I became certain that what was happening to me was more real than what the bishop or anyone else might witness with the eyes. To check this out, I asked my nurse when she came in, "Am I under any sort of heavy drugs?"

But she responded no, I was not on any drugs to speak of at that particular point. At about this time, I also experienced a turning point in my recovery and began to get much better. Later, when I was released from the hospital, I asked my doctor, "Was I very sick? Would you say I was in critical condition?"

"Yes," replied the doctor, who was a Muslim from India. "Many people were praying for you because that was all that we thought we could do. Even I was praying for you. I really thought we were going to lose you."

I'll never forget that floating sensation, because it provided me with a tremendous sense of freedom and happiness. As I pondered the meaning of the experience, I kept recalling what Paul had related about himself in 2 Corinthians 12:2: "I know a man in Christ who fourteen years ago was caught up to the third heaven—whether in the body or out of the body I do not know, God knows."

I wouldn't say that I was caught up to the third heaven. But I do feel that God was definitely at work in me in a physical sense, doing something to comfort me spiritually, heal my body, and save me from the jaws of death. An incident like this, taken with an ongoing, lifetime relationship with Christ, should be enough to convince anyone who experiences it that God is indeed in control, both in this life and in the next.

So my intimacy with Christ helps me know, beyond any doubt, that death is not the end. I have no fear of death whatsoever. Even when I'm confronted with the death of others, my first thought is usually not of the deceased, but of those who are still living. I wonder how they are reacting and how their lives may be changed. Death can strike great fear into a survivor's heart if that survivor has no understanding of a relationship with God.

I was deeply involved in a meeting with two other men when news of the terrible explosion of the *Challenger* space shuttle came to us. As we heard the report that the craft had blown up and all the astronauts had apparently been killed instantly, I couldn't believe it at first. I found it very difficult to accept the news. The event was so shocking, it almost seemed as though my heart stopped.

At that moment, I didn't think, "Who's to blame for

this?" Also, I didn't just focus on those who had died. Rather, I thought what a tragedy this was for those still living—for the nation, for humanity, and especially for the surviving spouses, children, and other family members. As I pondered the loss suffered by those people, I lapsed into silence. It made me extremely sad when I realized that there was little or nothing I could do to help them or respond to their terrible plight.

When I'm hearing someone express grief over the loss of a loved one and I realize all I can do is respond with words, I feel something deep inside that's closely akin to pain. Also, when I go to someone to express sympathy for a death, I usually say nothing. I just take the person's hand in my hand and let that act of touching serve as my condolence.

For similar reasons, I find it very difficult to give funeral sermons. As I said, I can chuckle when I think about my own funeral. But I see nothing at all funny in the funerals of others. I go through agony while I'm preaching during a funeral ceremony because I know those survivors listening to me are not prepared to hear ordinary spiritual messages. They're usually not ready to absorb words about immortality or the resurrection. All they know is that they've lost a loved one, and they're devastated.

Frequently, they are in a state of shock and gripped by a fear of the future. How will the widow or widower get by without the beloved spouse who has now passed on? How will the children cope without the presence and authority of the parent who watched over them and protected them? How will the survivor who doesn't know God grapple with the great fears gnawing at him about his own eternal destiny?

To respond to these concerns, I find I must rely not on mere words but on God. Only his Spirit can project into the hearts of others comforting messages that are beyond my poor powers of oratory. My listeners must know that I'm not putting on a performance for them. I'm not just fulfilling some ritualistic need to wind up another person's life. Rather, my only purpose is to serve as a channel for the mystical power of Christ. What these survivors need most is to feel his love in their lives. That's the only way that the fears nagging at them can be banished and that true hope for the future can become a reality.

17

Burnout

Burnout—the state of feeling exhausted, "flat," or uninspired by one's work or ministry—is a common complaint among the achievers in our society. The symptoms of burnout vary from person to person, and situation to situation. But there are a few common ingredients that help us recognize this pervasive problem.

For example, your job, volunteer project, or even spiritual ministry may have seemed interesting and exciting at first. But now, the zest and sense of adventure is gone. Every day is pretty much the same. Either there seem to be no mountains left to conquer, or those mountains and challenges seem to involve arduous toil instead of high adventure. Before your burnout, you may have been riding on a tremendous surge of energy for a year, five years, ten years, or even longer. But now, the energy has run out. You get the job done, but you're no longer swept along on a wave of exuberant enthusiasm. Life is all work, with very little fun and joy.

You're not even very interested in the people with whom you work and associate. Sure, you still have friends. But when someone with a problem asks you for help, your tendency is to turn the other way and run. You feel overloaded, as though your internal systems will "freeze" if you get any more responsibilities or duties to perform.

In short, you lack many or all of the "fruits of the Spirit," that St. Paul describes in his Letter to the Galatians: You lack the love, joy, peace, patience, and other personal virtues and exhilarating feelings that are essential to make life seem worth living.

Acting as a kind of "spiritual diagnostician" for myself over the years, I have identified this burnout malady in my own life on certain occasions. I've been "wiped out" in my work and ministry, seemingly unable to continue. The fruits of the Spirit have been missing, and I've sometimes wondered if they would ever return.

This burnout experience was particularly intense and debilitating for me at one point while I was serving as a priest in Boston. I had been ministering there for more than twelve years, with an extremely heavy workload. I found that I consistently had to work from 7:00 in the morning until 11:00 in the evening, every single day of the week. Having given all that I could possibly give, I found that I was left without any spiritual and emotional resources. In short, I was burned out.

The signs of my burnout were all too apparent. For one thing, when I would finish confession with someone, I found I often harbored a sense of inadequacy, or even shame, because I hadn't always been able to devote my entire being to the needs of the person I had just seen. Also, I found I was tempted to repeat ideas and concepts in my writing and in my sermons. Yet I knew even then that the repetitious person is an exhausted person. I've always preferred just to keep silent rather than to repeat the same thing over and over again.

Clearly, I needed to be renewed or refilled spiritually, and, fortunately, I had sensitive, understanding superiors. When I expressed my needs, the Patriarch Athenagoras decided to appoint me to the World Council of Churches in Geneva, Switzerland. But my trials weren't over yet. For reasons I couldn't understand at first, I had to confront even more serious personal challenges later that year.

First of all, my mother died, and I had to go through the emotionally wrenching experience of sitting with her at her bedside as she lay there, getting weaker and weaker before my very eyes. She had been my first mentor and spiritual support; now, I had to become hers.

Also, at about this same time, the Turks rioted in Turkey against the Greeks. Churches were raided, graves were opened and the corpses of our people were dragged out. As I walked through the poor sections of Istanbul with an American air attaché, I saw with my own eyes how the people's reserves of flour and sugar, along with their beds and blankets, had been thrown out into the streets. It was a persecution the likes of which I had never witnessed before, and which I sincerely hope I'll never see again.

Understandably, I wondered at first what God had in mind, exposing me to these challenges in my depleted spiritual state. Then, I found out. When I returned to Geneva after the death of my mother and after witnessing the inhumanities of the rioting mobs, I found that I had forgotten all about my own spiritual dryness and misery! Being deeply involved in another part of the world, with those who were much worse off than I, had cured me completely of the burnout that I had been experiencing.

One of the main things I learned from this experience is that I'm a very poor judge of what I need to be refilled and rejuvenated by God's Spirit. Only God himself, and those human beings he has selected as his representatives, possessed the wisdom to guide me to those places and circumstances that could fill me up once again with spiritual power.

Somehow, when I returned to Geneva in September of 1955, I was a different person. Deep inside, God had filled me with his Spirit and released dormant reservoirs of strength that I was not even aware I possessed. Even more mysterious to me was the specific way God had acted. Against all human wisdom, he had used a series of painful personal crises to trigger the release of those new spiritual energies. All I had done in this situation was recognize that I was weak. But somehow, that recognition on my part was all God needed to act in my life.

In this regard, I'm reminded of what St. Paul said in his Second Letter to the church at Corinth: He had asked God to rid him of a "thorn in the flesh," but God replied, "My grace is sufficient for you, for my power is made perfect in weakness." Paul then went on to conclude, rather paradoxically, "For when I am weak, then I am strong."

From the world's point of view, none of this may make any sense. But from God's point of view, these words make all the sense in the world: He wants us to know that he is the only one with the power to renew us and fill us with spiritual energy. He and he alone can overcome the exhaustion and burnout that human pressures inevitably inflict upon us.

In Boston, I had reached the end of my capabilities. I knew that I had done all that was humanly possible in the time allotted to me, but my efforts simply weren't enough. I was exhausted, unable to fulfill the requirements of my ministry. Also, I sensed I was all alone, facing a hopeless fight that I had no chance of winning.

But it was just this feeling that I was "at the end of my rope" that opened the door for God to act. I could never have delivered myself successfully from that state of exhaustion and burnout. But God had the power to rescue me. In ways that I never expected, he used personal crisis, tragedy, and a change of scene, not only to help me survive, but actually to make me stronger than I had been before.

Finally, I soon found that the fruits of the Spirit, which I had been sorely lacking during my final days in Boston, began to enter my life. It's easy just to list the fruits of the Spirit, as Paul does in Galatians 5:22–23: "Love, joy, peace, patience, kindness, goodness, faithfulness, gentleness, self-control. . . ." But it's not so easy to move from lists to real life. It's not so easy to make these fruits an abiding part of your daily existence.

Ultimately, the fruits of the Spirit come to us as a result of God's grace. By ourselves, we can't generate them or make them appear magically, just as we can't create bananas, oranges, or pears out of nothing.

Still, even after God provides the spiritual seeds, we'll only see the fruits of the Spirit ripen in our lives if we continue to abide in him. Abiding in him means we must experience and practice his presence during challenges such as "burnout," as well as during grief, tragedy, and suffering. As we learn to endure, God can teach us more about relying on him. Also, abiding in him involves pursuing spiritual disciplines, such as prayer, self-study, and Bible study.

In a sense, then, even though the fruits of the Spirit are

the product of God's grace, we have to work if we hope to see them develop. The appearance of God's fruit depends on what might be called "spiritual horticulture," or an ongoing effort to grow in God's grace and be transformed in the image of Christ. In my own case, I've preached on the fruits of the Spirit dozens of times, but it took me many long years before I really tasted them on a regular basis. Now, I enjoy love, peace, patience, and joy fairly consistently in my life. But for many years, I did not.

On the other hand, *you* may be able to enjoy the full flavor of these fruits of the Spirit much earlier than I did. With careful attention to "spiritual work," such as prayer and obedience to God's will for your life, you can begin to bear the fruits of the Spirit much sooner than you might expect.

But even as spiritual fruit begins to appear in your life, be realistic. Expect to keep working hard for God. Pray regularly, protect the gifts you've been given, and fight the "parasites" and "locusts" that lurk in the gardens of your daily life, waiting to destroy or devour God's fruits before you can pick them and put them on your table.

When you're exhausted or bored, and generally feel burned out with your daily routine and responsibilities, the ground of your life is not fertile for the growth of love, joy, peace, or gentleness. But when you are renewed and filled up by the Spirit, the time is near for the ripening of God's fruit. You're ready to savor the sweet smells and succulent tastes of the rich spiritual vineyards that God has made available for your enjoyment.

PART III

THE PUBLIC WAY

18

Unity in the Spirit:
The Ultimate Promise
of Human History

Tranquillity. Harmony. Peace among the peoples.

Throughout the ages, men and women have longed for a society that would embody the ideal, "One for all, and all for one." Treatises have been written to explain how this unity and understanding among humans might be achieved. Attempts have even been made to establish such communities.

But invariably, all the attempts have failed. All the good intentions have gone for naught. As the Lord said in the Book of Jeremiah, we cry " 'peace, peace,' when there is no peace."

We have failed miserably to achieve spiritual oneness and unity—whether in politics, voluntary interest groups, or religious denominations and organizations. Far from being unified or in harmony with one another, our relationships are characterized more by disputes and war than by peace. So many of our interactions with others are characterized by the "works of the flesh" that Paul lists in his Letter to the Galatians: enmity, strife, jealousy, anger, selfishness, dissension, factionalism.

One of the major obstacles to unity is that our values are mixed up. We march to the drumbeat of fragmented, conflict-producing technology rather than true spirituality. For thousands of years, people lived without resorting to the inventions and philosophies of technology. Yet today, our lives are controlled by mechanical devices and by the world views of technicians and scientists.

The so-called "burning" issues that we focus upon are deeply rooted in this technology: how to limit our ability to destroy ourselves with advanced weapons . . . how to teach the techniques of sex to both adults and children, so they can avoid diseases and pregnancies . . . how to perform abortions more easily and efficiently . . . how to conquer killer-diseases and improve our health so that we can live a few years longer . . . how to fine-tune our technology so that we can make our lives on earth a little easier and perhaps explore outer space more extensively.

Obviously, life today is different than it was in the time of Christ. We move faster, communicate more extensively, and, in some respects at least, seem to have more control over our environment. But as we increase our abilities in one area, we seem to lose them in another. As we make life easier on one level, we make it more likely we'll blow ourselves up or debase our humanity on another.

Still, through all this cultural confusion, the highest human aspirations toward unity and harmony remain the same. What we as a people desire most today is what human beings in every historical era have wanted: freedom, dignity, justice, equality, and peace. Yet still, we cry "peace" when there is no peace! We've lost our moorings. We've lost our sense of historical continuity and basic truth, and are drifting endlessly and aimlessly.

Perhaps the greatest losers in the fragmentation and decline of our culture and morality have been our children. Through near-criminal neglect, we've robbed them of their spiritual birthright. When I think of the plight of our children, I'm reminded of the encounter between the Greek philosopher Diogenes and Alexander the Great, when Alexander moved to a position between Diogenes and the sun. As the great conqueror shaded the philosopher from the solar rays, Diogenes said, "Don't take away something you cannot give—the sun."

Today, we are in a similar situation with our young people. We are taking away from them something we cannot give —namely, their innocence. We expose them to all manner of violence and sex and the fearful prospect of nuclear annihilation, all in the name of realism and education. Also, through divorce, overwork, and other insidious trends in the adult world, we separate our youngsters from what they need most: a close-knit, nurturing family, with parents who are available and capable of teaching eternal values.

After childhood has passed, there is no way to recapture lost innocence or the opportunity to have a malleable young personality shaped by the Spirit, rather than the world. By such neglect, we succeed in magnifying our own flaws and failings as we pass them on to the next generation. And with such neglect, there's no hope to strengthen the spiritual underpinnings necessary for peace and unity among peoples.

So what can we do about all this? Is the situation hopeless, or is there some possibility of reestablishing our basic values—and achieving some semblance of spiritual unity?

The road ahead is arduous, and sometimes the challenges will seem overwhelming and insurmountable. But still, I believe there is hope—*if* we take at least three key steps to change our way of acting and thinking.

Specifically, we first need to focus more on the human soul than on human society. Secondly, we must recognize that our culture doesn't exist in a vacuum, but is a product of important historical forces. Finally, we must commit ourselves, both as individuals and a total body of believers, to follow the footsteps of Jesus. Only through such a strategy can we hope to approach the unity in the Spirit which is our ultimate goal.

FOCUS ON THE HUMAN SOUL

In all sectors of our society—including Christian society —I perceive a willingness to deal with issues, doctrines, and institutions, but a tremendous reluctance to deal directly with the human soul. We rush to mold groups of people together into organizations, communities, and societies, and we expect them to function with near-perfect precision and selflessness, long before they really know who they are or what their basic purpose in life should be. We ignore the weaknesses and flaws of human nature unredeemed by the power of Christ.

To be sure, many Christians are willing to focus on the needs of individuals. For example, there is an emphasis in some Christian circles on promoting racial equality. Those involved often not only work through political and social movements, but also establish friendships and relationships with those of other ethnic backgrounds.

Also, a growing number of Christians are interested in "liberating" the poor and oppressed in various Third World societies. Here, again, those Christians who are trying to help may get involved directly with those whom they're trying to assist.

Finally, other believers may stress the importance of evangelism. They may work hard to lead those who have not made a commitment to Christ into a relationship with the Savior. Then, they'll set up Bible studies, prayer groups, and counseling sessions to help the new Christians grow in the faith.

In all such cases, the motives of the Christians, and many of their results are commendable. But still, those involved are often primarily interested in influencing large numbers of people or in pushing certain theological or political viewpoints. They're only secondarily interested in spending the time and energy necessary to help the single individual. Their first impulse is to tend to the group, not immerse themselves in the welfare of another needy human being.

I must confess that I myself have not always cared primarily for individual human souls. Furthermore, I feel very sad that I've neglected this task, because I know now that doctrines, theologies, and social and political philosophies mean nothing if the individuals in the group or society are lost. Yet to save a human soul, to work with an individual so that he or she grows up into the image of Christ, requires great commitment, patience, and humility. Too often, those who focus on broad, global movements and achievements simply lack the time and energy necessary to nurture the one needy man or woman.

To care for the individual human soul, it's necessary to spend hours at a bedside in a hospital . . . listen to the outpourings of one who is suffering emotional pain . . . serve food and offer uplifting words from Christ day after day, week after week to those who are in need . . . visit elderly relatives regularly—and that may mean weekly or even daily—in their nursing homes . . . spend minutes, hours, or days explaining the Gospel to uncommitted spiritual searchers . . . postpone what *you* had planned to do, and allow yourself to be guided by God into *his* chosen areas of service.

Caring for the individual human soul is, in many respects, a "messy" business. You may, quite literally, have to get your hands dirty as you care for a seriously ill friend, or guide a homeless person to a place of rest for the night. You may have to reschedule or even give up some of your own social activities in order to counsel a neighbor in anguish. You may have to set another place at your table, so that you can feed an emotionally or physically needy friend.

In the last analysis, caring for the single human soul must become our major occupation. It mustn't just be something we do sporadically or in certain slots in our schedules, perhaps to help salve our consciences. After all, Jesus' entire life and ministry were spent stopping, responding, and changing his plans in order to meet the needs and demands of those around him. He even interrupted his own prayer times with the Father in order to respond to Peter and others who craved his presence.

As servants of Christ, we are not greater than our Master, who was the greatest Servant of all. His service focused not so much on large groups or issues, as on loving individual human beings, on loving single, solitary souls. Only when he had responded to those specific persons and concerns was the way paved for his followers to join hands in unified action and understanding. In short, then, we must concentrate on the deepest spiritual needs of the individual before we can hope to make a beginning that will lead us into an authentic circle of spiritual unity.

LOOK FOR HARMONY IN HISTORY

If you first immerse yourself in serving others and truly learn to love them, you'll then be in a much better position to understand broader concepts and trends. And I do believe that ultimately, you *must* study what has gone before—that is, the history of humanity—in order to achieve some measure of unity among groups of people.

For example, I could never comment intelligently on the current obsession with technology if I didn't understand that our mechanistic, technological mindset is a relatively recent phenomenon. History teaches us that we can get along quite well without technology. Faith and other spiritual values hardly depend upon what kind of car you drive, how many gadgets you have in your home, or what the outlook is for the next generation of computers.

As I study the history of the human race, I also see an ongoing concern about and search for God. I see individual men and women struggling to understand the meaning of their lives, struggling to live at peace with one another and struggling to find the truth that undergirds their existence. In short, I see them struggling to know who God is and how he is at work in this world.

Of course, the kind of history I'm talking about here is not just a list of dates or a description of a series of events. Rather, the only history that abides is a history of human beings—the histories, for instance, that Herodotus, Thucydides, Plutarch, and other classic historians passed on to us. The best historians have tried to describe to us how individual men and women responded to the demands of war, political upheaval, and social unrest. Oftentimes, the ancient historians

also brought in references to the religious and spiritual implications of historical happenings, including the way they believed the pagan gods had an impact on various trends and
events.

The history of Christianity fits quite naturally into this
broad understanding of reality—but with some clear differences. Certainly, the Bible and other Christian writings describe major movements of people, wars, and dramatic inci-
dents involving key leaders. But throughout the Scriptures, we
are also presented with an ongoing account of how God has
interacted with men and women and has imposed his will and
overall plan on human events.

Some of the greatest moments of human history are contained in the records of the Hebrew people and of Christianity.
What today can compare with the Passover events in Egypt, or
the parting of the Red Sea for Moses and the Israelites? And
can you imagine a more significant and uplifting event than
the nativity of Christ, the entry of God himself into human
history through the incarnation?

But at the same time, the Old and New Testaments, as
well as subsequent Christian historical accounts, contain some
of the low points of the human historical record.

Consider St. Stephen, the first martyr, who delivered his
great sermon in Acts 7, just before he was stoned to death. In
that speech, he charged that the history of the Hebrew people,
God's chosen nation, had been more a history of disobedience
than of obedience to the divine will. The Hebrews had consistently rejected their leaders, their prophets, and even God
himself.

Then, as St. Stephen delivered his indictments and was
stoned, the Pharisee Saul, one of the future leaders of the
Christian church, stood to one side, watching the garments of

those who were killing the martyr. When Saul, later known as Paul, finally assumed leadership in the Christian church, he found the sad tradition of disobedience and human failure wasn't by any means limited to himself or the Hebrews. He had to speak out regularly against immorality and faithlessness among those who were members of the new congregations he helped to establish.

The disappointments, difficulties, and scandals also continued unabated after the close of the biblical era. To mention just a few, there were wars between those who favored the use of icons in the church, and the "iconoclasts" who opposed them. There was the Inquisition in Spain, with its excommunications and persecutions. The annals of later Christian history are also littered with sinful acts of church leaders and murder after murder committed in the name of Christ.

Even today, we are tasting the bitter fruits of factionalism and dissension. St. Paul said in his Letter to the Romans that the Holy Spirit sometimes "groans" with sighs that are too deep for words. Today, too, there is just such a groaning among our young people and also among many concerned adults. The Spirit is speaking through our people, crying out for religious leaders to return to their historical roots, to take the reins and guide society in more productive directions. Unfortunately, however, too few of the mature clergy and laity are assuming leadership. Instead of being bold enough to listen and respond to the groaning of the Spirit, they follow the standards of the corrupt secular culture.

Too many Christian leaders—products of unbelieving, Enlightenment philosophies—are utilitarians about society's values, in much the same way that our secular leaders are utilitarians. They evaluate issues on rationalistic, rather than spiritual, grounds. They compile lists of arguments for and against abortion, for and against homosexuality, for and against a variety of other social and political issues. Instead of simply proclaiming the truth from a biblical and historical perspective—instead of saying that abortion is wrong or that a homosexual lifestyle is contrary to God's will—they seek sociological and political justifications.

In short, we Christians have lost our prophetic voice—in part because we have lost our sense of our history. We have in front of us a sick society. But instead of moving decisively to cure it, as Jesus and St. Paul did, we toss weak words back and forth; then, we move on to discuss some other abstract topic. Instead of joining hands to counter the evil in our midst and to make God's will a reality, we posture and squabble and present a fractured front to the world.

The same kind of utilitarian disputation characterizes Christian ecumenical conferences. Rationalistic theologians and lukewarm denominational leaders split hairs in trying to forge some sort of institutional and organizational unity. And sometimes, these negotiating sessions do result in some points of compromise and settlements.

But usually, such settlements are little more than religious first-aid patches that do little more than temporarily relieve the superficial symptoms of a more serious underlying spiritual disease. Too often, those participating in ecumenical meetings lack the fire and zeal necessary to cut through superficial institutional issues and get right to the heart of the spiritual malaise.

On the other hand, those who may possess this zeal, such as certain Protestant fundamentalists and evangelicals, often close themselves off from the broader ecumenical movements. If they would open their doors and share more fully and lovingly with their fellow Christians of other denominations, they might enhance the possibility for real Christian unity.

As we consider the events of the past and their impact on the present, it all may seem rather discouraging and shameful. We may even be tempted to ignore the devastating historical record of how men and women have strayed far from the will of God. Yet we must force ourselves to look at these accounts of what's gone before. We must study them and try to understand them. Only by exploring what went right *and* wrong in the past can we hope to see what our problems are today—and perhaps discover a way to work together and achieve unity under God's love in the future.

SIT AT THE FEET OF THE SAGES

History should become a kind of "classroom" where we can learn important lessons from the past, which will help us in practical ways in the present. In a sense, we can "sit at the feet" of the sages of bygone eras and benefit as they teach us in their recorded words and actions.

It's quite appropriate, then, that the English word "history" comes from a Greek word meaning "I know." In fact, a major purpose of history is to increase our knowledge of the reality around us, and especially the reality of God. Also, history can teach us how to bring people into harmony and how to avoid the pitfalls that aggravate tensions and dissension.

But if we study history without first understanding the role of God in human affairs, then what we read will probably make relatively little sense—and certainly won't be very useful. Of course, intelligent people can always pick out trends and concepts that impose some semblance of order on the countless events of the past. But still, without God, I'm afraid that our history reading must lead us to say with Socrates, "I know one thing, that I know nothing."

Yet when God is present to help us integrate and interpret facts and trends, history becomes more meaningful and usable. Also, the more Christ-centered we are as we read history—even history that seems to have nothing to do with Christianity or the church—the better we can understand the possibilities of spiritual unity, including the viability of various strategies to spread the Gospel.

Consider the way that Paul dealt with the different cultures in the Greek cities of his day. Athens was an intellectually sophisticated city, much like today's Boston, and Paul accommodated his preaching style to deal with this peculiarity. Certainly, his ultimate goal was always the same wherever he preached: to bring as many people as possible into the new, unified life offered by Christ. But he tailored his oratorical technique so as to appeal to the special needs and interests of each audience. So in Athens, being a student of Hellenistic philosophy and culture, he quoted from the Stoic poets in his sermon on Mars Hill. Also, he used the altar "to an unknown god" in Athens as his point of departure to talk about Christ.

Then, when Paul traveled from Athens to Corinth, he changed his approach, perhaps partly because Corinth had a different culture from Athens. Corinth was a more affluent city, with a significant commercial base and seaport, and the social life there was quite active and unusually immoral. The Corinthians—perhaps like today's New Yorkers or even Dallasites—were more materialistic and less academically oriented than the Athenians. So Paul decided to deliver a simpler, more straightforward message in Corinth: He tells us in his First Letter to the Corinthians that he resolved to preach

"Jesus Christ and him crucified" and not to rely on words of worldly wisdom.

Paul's missionary work also provides other lessons for us today. For example, in Athens, Corinth, and elsewhere, Paul began his ministry by focusing on the synagogues, where the worshipers included both Hellenistic Jews and "God-fearers," or non-Jews who were interested in the Hebrew religion. Then, after he had preached and taught to those who were most likely to be familiar with and receptive to his message, he branched out into the community at large. In Athens and Corinth he preached to those Greeks who might have known nothing about the Jewish Messiah, but who still were responsive to Paul's ability to communicate the message of salvation to them on their own terms.

So what can we learn from this little bit of history?

I believe Paul has given us a model missionary strategy, one that should encourage us to focus on domestic and sophisticated urban missions rather than on many foreign missions. Today, many churches and Christian organizations prefer going abroad—or at least away from home—to spread the truth of Christ among undeveloped nations and peoples. Yet if we look closely at our great urban centers, such as New York, Paris, London, or Tokyo, we'll find that the Gospel really hasn't penetrated very deeply.

So perhaps we should take the cue from St. Paul and rethink our approach to spreading the Gospel. Perhaps we should give a priority to those dead or dying churches in our large cities, which are in some respects like the synagogues of the Diaspora—or those outside the Holy Land during Paul's day. Then, after these churches have been revitalized, they will be in a position to serve as bases to spread the message to those on the highways and byways of their communities.

Perhaps, too, we should be inspired by Paul's vast knowledge of the philosophy and culture of his day. How powerfully he was able to communicate the Gospel in the cultural terms of his listeners! Paul preferred to convince, rather than convert. He didn't bludgeon and bully with his message. With incisive logic and rhetoric, he went directly to the point of the people's greatest need. Then, he proceeded to persuade them that the path of Jesus was the one that they should follow.

St. Paul's adventures in Athens, Corinth, and elsewhere always have the power to make me rethink the present, and they inspire me as I formulate my spiritual strategies for the future. When I consider Paul's work, or other past trends and events, I ask myself, "What does this mean for me now, today? How can I apply to the present what I've learned about the events and movements of the past?"

Then, as I begin to see the continuity between the needs of the individual and the lessons of history, I'm in a better position to understand and work toward that spiritual unity, which Jesus has called us to experience.

FOLLOW IN THE FOOTSTEPS OF JESUS

Without Jesus Christ there can be no true unity in the Spirit. Indeed, Christianity is nothing more or less than a movement comprised of those who have decided to walk, by faith, in his footsteps.

Jesus didn't come to earth to teach us a set of doctrines or concepts. Nor did he leave behind a particular body of knowledge or some systematic theology. He didn't even come to teach us truth. As you'll recall, when Jesus was asked by Pilate, "What is truth?" he didn't reply. I believe the reason he kept quiet is that his primary aim was not to raise such inte, lectual questions in human minds. Rather, he came to resurrect the human heart. He came to inspire and motivate us to be filled up with God's Spirit, to follow the Spirit's impulse toward perfection and immortality.

Unfortunately, however, the "center of gravity" of our culture has shifted from the spiritual to the material. Marxists and capitalists alike have been quite successful because they have managed to get most of us, whatever our politics or national backgrounds, to be interested primarily in the here and now. They urge us to focus on the physical things that we can touch, taste, and smell.

But Jesus challenges us on a deeper level. He said that we can't survive by bread alone, but that we need spiritual nourishment. He told us to reorder our priorities; to push aside our primary emphasis on our food, clothing, and worldly riches; and to seek first the Kingdom of God.

Once we reorder our priorities in this way, we'll still have to deal with the material necessities of life. But at least our interest in them shouldn't consume us. They should occupy a healthier, better-balanced place in our lives, as we allow God to conform us gradually, over many years of spiritual growth, to the image of his Son.

The footsteps of Jesus may take us many places we've never expected to go, from the precarious mountains to the meadows, from the meadows to the seashore, and from the seashore back to the mountains again. His steps will take us from prayer to love, from love to suffering, and from suffering to crucifixion.

But regardless of the heights or depths that we reach on this path, we can be certain that Jesus will always be present,

sure not only our survival but also our tri-
promised us his Spirit to provide us with the
guidance we need to discover true unity with God
others.

19

The Joy of Koinonia

One of the most exciting things I've witnessed in recent years is the movement among lay people to get together once a week to pray and share deep concerns. Such groups are active in the United States Senate, in the House of Representatives, in many major corporations, in private clubs, and in homes throughout the land.

The people who participate in these gatherings are not interested in deep philosophical or intellectual discussions. Rather, they come together because they love Christ and want to learn more about loving one another. Also, most of them are needy people. It's not so much that they need money or the material things of life. Rather, they need emotional and spiritual support and nurturance.

The participants are men and women with family problems, financial worries, career anxieties, and burdens of grief, which sometimes seem too hard to bear. Yet when they join

together and begin to share their concerns with one another—
and especially when they open their hearts to God in prayer—
they find their needs being met. Healings take place, and they
become much stronger individuals, able not only to receive
help but to give it as well.

Such groups are wonderful expressions of an experience
that has been essential to Christian growth and development
over the centuries—the experience of *koinonia.* The New Testament word *koinonia* is variously translated as "fellowship,"
"community," or "togetherness." Where true *koinonia* is present, there is excitement, enhanced individual spiritual growth,
and greater joy in our lives.

But in practical terms, what exactly is involved in *koinonia?*

St. Paul refers many times in his epistles to the purposes
and signs of *koinonia.* He says in his First Letter to the Thessalonians that *koinonia* will cause us to encourage one another
. . . build one another up . . . exhort the brethren . . . ad-
monish the idle . . . encourage the fainthearted . . . help
the weak . . . be patient with all . . . and pray for one another.

The only way we can relate to one another in this way is
to stay in close contact and grow together under the leadership
of Christ. For this reason, I think *koinonia* can best be understood as living together in Christ, or living together in the
fellowship of the Holy Spirit.

Yet today, we value our privacy and independence. The
idea of "living together" with somebody outside our families,
or exposing our inner selves to them, or submitting to their
spiritual authority can be extremely disturbing, if not repug-
nant. But such personal exposure and transparency in the
company of others is what *koinonia* is all about.

It's very difficult to understand this kind of relationship in terms of most of our human contacts. When we put together a volunteer organization, a business or a United Nations, we're really not "united" in the deepest sense of the word. Rather, such organizations—even when they're broken down into "working committees"—are usually comprised of individuals with quite different philosophies of life and personal interests. The only thing that binds them together is the common purpose and ethos of the organization. This means that as a group, they're limited in terms of any consensus that they can reach on nonbusiness matters, or in the personal relationships that they can foster.

In *koinonia,* in contrast, it's not an organization—not even the institutional church—that binds the individuals together. Rather, the "glue" that causes one individual to adhere to another for long periods of time, if not for life, is a supernatural, spiritual force. It's a cohesive power that we can only begin to understand as we partake in the very nature of Christ through Holy Communion and then relate daily to one another as spiritual brothers and sisters.

True *koinonia,* then, begins with a living participation in the life of the risen Christ. Then, as you pursue this personal partaking in the life of Christ, it's natural to reach out and join hands with others who also share in his Spirit. Yet this sharing, down-to-earth as it may be at times, does not occur just on a human level. Certainly, you can "share" your food or your lawn mower with someone who doesn't relate to God in the same way that you do. But to achieve real *koinonia,* it's necessary for there to be a unity of purpose and experience. The togetherness of *koinonia* is possible because true Christians have many important things in common: They share the same faith, the same goals, and the same pattern of life. Most important of all, they share Jesus, who binds human to human in spiritual togetherness. Without him, there can be no *koinonia*.

But when he is present, the outlook for spiritual unity is practically limitless. Consider just a few of the possibilities:

- When Jesus said, "My peace I give unto you, not as the world gives, give I unto you," he was pointing the way toward a harmony in relationships that is only possible in him.

- When we pray, "Thy kingdom come," we are saying together that we have God's hope that we will be bound together, throughout eternity, with Christ.

- When we sing "Faith of Our Fathers" or "What a Friend We Have in Jesus," our voices well up together, not just in musical harmony but in spiritual accord as well.

The togetherness of *koinonia*, then, is a togetherness in God's Spirit. It's a Communion that transcends all human understanding and earthly limitations.

On a personal level, I find that when I'm engaged in *koinonia*, my spirit is renewed in ways that would be impossible otherwise. During Holy Week, for example, I draw new strength from those dear Christians with whom I talk and engage in worship. From Palm Sunday through Easter, I spend extra time with God in prayer, but also extra time with other people in fellowship.

By all rights, as I've indicated before, I should be debilitated by fatigue because of the extra responsibilities during this time of the year. But in fact, *koinonia* enables me to overcome that physical tiredness. The nurturance of others helps me to go beyond the limitations of my human body and savor a deep inner joy, which is one of the most precious gifts of God's Spirit. And as I reflect on such experiences, I realize that a large part of my rejoicing arises from worshiping and sharing with others, who give praises to that same Lord who rules all our lives.

20

The Dialogue Imperative

Reflect for a moment on how major changes and insights have taken place in your life.

What were the circumstances under which you decided to get married . . . selected your present career . . . chose your method of child-rearing . . . or settled upon your personal approach to religious faith and practice?

The chances are you didn't make any of these decisions only on the basis of hearing an inspiring lecture, sermon, or lesson in a classroom. Certainly, what you may have heard from an inspiring speaker could have been quite influential and may even have triggered your final decision. But most likely, there was also a great deal of prior thought and conversation with others that preceded these life-changing moments and choices.

As far as our religious commitments are concerned, we may see people on television or in large rallies go forward when the evangelist gives an "altar call," or when he urges a "decision for Christ" or some other life-changing choice. But more often than not, a considerable amount of thought and interaction with other people have occurred before these decisions ever take place.

In Billy Graham's evangelistic campaigns, for example, months and even years of prayer and planning precede the week or two of sermons which he delivers. Also, individual Graham campaign workers spend a great deal of time publicizing the event and inviting prospective converts to the meetings. Finally, after the altar call has been given, those who have come forward meet with counselors so they can discuss their emotional and spiritual concerns and confirm their commitments.

In fact, the most effective evangelistic campaigns have always been conducted in this fashion. During the period of the Great Awakening in the early eighteenth century in the American colonies, the evangelist-preacher Jonathan Edwards delivered many sermons during which scores of people made on-the-spot commitments to follow Christ. But in fact, studies of the historical records reveal that a considerable number of conversations and discussions about the upcoming evangelistic meetings often occurred to pave the way for the sermons.

The point that I'm getting at here is this: In most cases, we independent-minded and often stubborn human beings need more than a stirring lecture or sermon to change our lives. Most of us are not, by nature, passive, docile creatures. We want to interact, respond, and participate in our search for the answer to life's big and little questions. We want to "say our piece" and make our viewpoints known to others. In short, most of us would much rather talk than listen! And even those who are quiet or shy still usually harbor strong opinions that can't be changed too easily by others.

I think God has always understood this human inclination to want to take a strong position on important matters and resist being pushed into a new set of beliefs or practices by anyone, including God himself. So the prophet Isaiah quotes God, who says to his stubborn human children, "Come now, let us reason together." (Isaiah 1:18, RSV)

God knows that we are most responsive to the overtures of truth when we can engage in conversation or dialogue, either with him or with other people. Jesus made many of his most effective points when he asked questions or engaged in intense discussions with his disciples or various spiritual searchers. A book could be written just on probing questions like these:

To his disciples: "Who do the people say that I am?"

To the Pharisee Nicodemus: "Are you a teacher of Israel, and yet you do not understand this?"

To his parents: "Did you not know that I must be in my Father's house?"

To Peter in the Garden of Gethsemane: "So, could you not watch with me one hour?"

Questions, intense interactions, deep dialogues—these were key features of Jesus' ministry on earth. Yet today, we have lost the art of spiritual dialogue. Preachers speak from a special pulpit apart from their congregations, and the congregations sit in passive, often sleepy rows, trying to absorb what the speaker is saying. But there is no interaction, no personal involvement, no give-and-take, one with the other.

What a contrast when we compare our present situation with Jesus talking with the Samaritan woman at the well! In an ongoing dialogue with this woman, he helped her to understand herself. He didn't just speak *to* her: Rather, he interacted *with* her.

Also, when Jesus' disciples or some of the religious leaders of his day criticized him for eating and drinking with tax collectors and prostitutes, he didn't ignore their criticisms. Rather, he acknowledged their disapproval and then met them on their own grounds in conversation until the issues had been resolved.

When the mother of the disciples John and James approached Jesus about sitting on the Savior's right and left when he came into his Kingdom, he didn't ignore the request or belittle it. Instead, he used their request as a starting point to discuss some important principles about the Kingdom of God.

Human beings have been created in such a way that they need to interact and communicate with one another and with God in order to experience great changes in their lives. Yet we set up our classrooms and religious sanctuaries in such a way that people are unable to engage in the dialogues which they so desperately need. Preaching is certainly one way to minister to people, but I don't think it's the best or most effective. I'd prefer to go back to the example of Jesus or even Socrates, who was one of the most perceptive men of all time, though he functioned outside the biblical tradition.

The philosopher Plato, who recorded the dialogues of Socrates, said that Socrates "brought God down to earth." His method was based on a "peripatetic philosophy," which involved walking around with a student and asking penetrating questions to encourage the student to find his own path to truth.

Socrates understood, quite wisely, that neither he nor any other teacher, no matter how scintillating or qualified, could impose a system of truth or any ultimate answer to life's questions on another person. Rather, it was necessary for the person to find truth by himself. Socrates saw himself as using a system of intellectual and spiritual "midwifery" in order to help the other person "give birth" to profound ideas and make life-changing decisions.

This great Greek believed that deep inside the individual there were faculties that gave each person access to the *logos,* or the underlying rational and meaningful structure of all reality. All that a good teacher was supposed to do was to ask questions and point the way so that the individual student could conduct his own search and find truth for himself.

In some respects, we have a similar situation in the Christian faith. We believe that once a person has established a relationship with Jesus Christ, the power of the Holy Spirit is available in that person's life. But to walk in the way of faith and learn the truths that can only be conveyed by the Spirit, it's necessary for the individual to find his own way, under the guidance of God. All that other human beings can do is ask probing questions and suggest new directions and approaches.

Ultimately, no one else can live the life of faith for us. We hear about God through others; and we can even hear God himself in the prophetic words of fellow believers, prophets, and preachers. But in the final analysis, it's up to each of us, as individuals, to respond. And I believe that a productive response is most likely to take place as a result of dialogue.

I was deeply impressed with the importance of dialogue in communicating the Gospel message when I spoke to a group of businessmen out in Salt Lake City a couple of years ago. Most were accustomed to having preachers and lecturers speak to them, answer very few or no questions, and then leave them to figure out the answers for themselves.

But in our meeting, I tried a different approach. I devoted most of my time to listening to the concerns and complaints of the business people and to answering their questions. I really enjoyed the interaction, and I found I was learning a great deal myself during the discussion. But I wasn't aware of the impact on my listeners until after the session was finished. One of the men came up to me and said, "You know, this is the first time that my faith has seemed to have a content that really interested me!"

I'm sure that this man had heard many good sermons in his life. But his problem, like that of many people, was that he had never been given the opportunity to interact with the speaker. He had never asked the specific questions and made the special observations that were important to him personally and to the development of his faith.

Nor was this man an isolated example. His attitudes and experience are repeated over and over again among church members and spiritual inquirers in every part of the country. Unfortunately, however, our worship services are not usually set up in such a way that these specific individual needs can be met.

How can we correct this problem? I'd suggest that we take a cue from the current-issue television and radio talk shows that are so popular these days. Of course, there are many problems with these shows: In many cases, the hosts on these shows confuse people or lead them in unproductive directions, mainly because the hosts themselves often don't know where they're going.

But Christian leaders, both clergy and laity, can put some of these provocative question-and-answer techniques to good use. With a little thought and adjustment of the TV hosts' style, they should be able to inspire deeper thinking and help guide others in following the footsteps of Jesus.

Specifically, we need incisive discussion leaders who can help people with their family problems, with their marriage difficulties, and with their questions about careers and the management of their money. These leaders must grapple with such issues as, What's the Christian approach to marriage? To money? How do we find God's will in our daily lives?

Certainly, there *are* answers to these and similar questions. But in most cases, the best answers won't be communicated through lectures and sermons. Rather, we can only get to the heart of the matter, to the specifics that tailor an answer to a given person's situation, through dialogue.

In practical terms, though, how might this work be done in the pulpit? There are a number of useful approaches, some of which are already in use in a number of churches. For example, a preacher might go ahead and preach a normal sermon, just to lay the groundwork for discussing certain important issues. But he shouldn't stop there. After the service, he might provide a time for questions and answers—that is, for dialogue—so that his listeners will have a chance to respond to the points that he has made.

The preacher will undoubtedly not have covered every aspect of the topic that he has chosen in the twenty or thirty minutes allotted for his sermon. So in a small or medium-sized congregation, an "ask-the-priest" or "ask-the-minister" session after the service can provide an ideal forum to allow members of the congregation to get their specific concerns out on the table. In larger churches, the congregation might be divided into smaller groups to pursue such discussions under the direction of several members of the clergy or qualified lay leaders.

Another way to promote dialogue in our churches is to establish small discussion groups apart from the sermon presentations. These groups might focus on Bible study, or they might involve *koinonia*-type prayer-and-share meetings. In any event, the participants should be allowed an opportunity to raise questions that are bothering them. During these sessions, they can learn from members of the clergy or laity, who are more experienced Christians, how they may approach a pressing concern in their lives.

St. Basil the Great, one of the great Fathers of the Church who has been influential in my own spiritual development and ministry, said that you can't be a good preacher unless you "raise an interest in all the congregation." In other words, if you don't get people involved in what you're saying—so involved that they're encouraged to *act* on your words—then you're a failure.

In part, this means that we shouldn't preach or teach over the heads of our church members. We need to deal with issues that are relevant to the everyday life of each Christian. To achieve this end, it's absolutely necessary to give every lay person an opportunity to engage in a spiritual dialogue that will allow the exploration of possible answers to particular personal problems.

Many times, as we open up the possibility of discussion and dialogue among believers and searchers, the conversation may stray quite far from the topics that we expected. Also, more often than not, the leader of the discussion will be surprised by the questions that are put to him.

When I was discussing spiritual matters with one group of families, a little three-year-old boy asked one of the most disconcerting, yet important questions of the day. During a lull in the adult conversation, he asked, "Tell me about God. Does God talk to you?"

That question enabled me to shift the discussion from an abstract, impersonal level to a more intimate interchange. I was given an opening to tell this group of people in very simple terms exactly what God means to me.

On another occasion, after I had delivered a rather difficult address on a fine point of theology, an elderly man came up after I had finished speaking and asked, "Are you a theologian?"

"No, I'm not," I replied. "I studied theology, but I'm not a theologian."

"I wonder how important it is to understand a great deal about theology?" he continued. "For example, I've heard speakers discuss mathematical arguments which are supposed to show us that God really exists. But I wonder if God is really like that? Does his existence really need to be proven that way? A God of philosophy seems to me to be a God who is far beyond my understanding. Or maybe such a God is not so powerful after all, if he needs smart human beings to prove to other humans that he exists! What do you think?"

I immediately agreed with him, and I felt somewhat chastened at having emphasized in my talk some difficult points of theology. Like this man, I feel that a God who needs human sophistication and intellectual expertise isn't really God at all. The God I know is the all-powerful, personal Being whom I feel inside me, whom I believe in and trust. I don't have to argue him into existence. As I live with him day by day, I become completely convinced of his existence through practical experience.

I'm always grateful for these opportunities to engage in dialogue because if I didn't have people like this little boy and this old man to keep my feet firmly planted in reality, I might quickly lose touch with the actual needs of other people. For that matter, without such dialogue I would lose touch with my *own* needs. God speaks to me through these discussions and interactions as much as he does to those who are asking the questions.

And as they ask and I answer—or I ask and they answer —we explore and discover together new dimensions of truth. Important new insights thus tend *not* to be imposed on us from without. Rather, through spiritual dialogue, we search and find the answers deep within ourselves. The Christian *Logos*— or the "Word," who is Jesus Christ himself—reveals himself to us deep inside our spirits as we conduct these explorations and discussions. And the answers we are finally given are the kind of answers that can influence us over a lifetime. They are the answers that can change our very beings and move us into a deeper relationship with Christ. Indeed, the answers that arise from dialogues with God and his people grasp and transform not only our minds, but our hearts as well.

21

Marriage: A Most Marvelous Sacrament

For me, marriage is one of the most important sacraments.

Why do I, a celibate clergyman, believe marriage is so important? First of all, the power of Christian *koinonia,* of community and fellowship, radiates outward, from small groups and relationships into society as a whole. At the center of this rippling series of relational waves, the smallest, and I believe most important, "group," the unit at the heart of all important human relationships, is the married couple. As a husband and wife join together in mystical, God-inspired union, they form the most fundamental building block used by God as he builds his Kingdom on this earth.

Also, a natural and absolutely essential outgrowth of the marriage relationship is the children it produces. If God is present in the union of the married couple, he will also be present in the growth and development of the sons and daughters who complete the immediate family.

Furthermore, as faith is passed on from generation to generation, there are grandparents and grandchildren, as well as aunts, uncles, and other relatives, who become part of the spiritual family network. Together, the blood relatives in these believing, extended families become the "living stones" that St. Peter says in his first epistle constitute God's "spiritual house," which has Jesus himself as the cornerstone.

One of the best examples I've encountered of how a good marriage can encourage a spiritually strong family network emerged recently in some of the simple, ordinary activities of a friend of mine. This man holds a very important position, and he could easily have delegated some of his family responsibilities to other people, or perhaps hire sitters or representatives to do his jobs for him. But he has chosen to tend to his family relationships himself because he regards them as extremely important.

So he regularly goes to visit his ninety-year-old mother, who is unable to get around by herself. In a typical gesture of his love for her, he even spent one weekend driving her miles away to a church that she had attended as a young woman. She had expressed a desire to visit the place once again, for old time's sake, before she died.

It would have been easy for this man to make up some excuse about why it was not a good idea for his mother to make this trip. He could have emphasized how busy he was at work, or he could have given some other reasonable explanation, such as saying that she was too weak and the trip might not be good for her. But instead, he put aside his own concerns and went out of his way to serve his mother in a way that would make her happy.

Nor is the Christian influence in this man's family limited to the older generation. The faith that he and his wife enjoy gets communicated quite clearly to his children, so much so that they have become spiritually precocious at a young age. His ten-year-old son, for example, recently came on his own to see me. The boy had a particular problem that was bothering him, and when we had closed the doors to my office, he prostrated himself in front of me. He then asked for my hand and said, "Please, say a prayer for me."

Such a young person wouldn't usually develop this kind of faith on his own. I see a strong parental influence here, a channeling of God's grace through the parents into the family and the lives of each of the children. Clearly, the strength of this spiritual house—which St. Peter also calls a "holy priesthood," a "holy nation," and "God's own people"—rests on the inner strength of the married couple. And the strength of the couple rests on their commitment to God.

Without the presence of God's Spirit, marriage ceases to be a sacrament. The living together of the husband and wife becomes a physical, rather than mystical or spiritual, communion. Without the sacramental ingredient, without the presence of God's grace, divine power disappears from the marriage, and God's spiritual house on this earth begins to crumble.

So you can see why I regard the sacrament of marriage as so important. The stability of our Christian communities—and even of our broader secular society—depends on the strength of the marriage relationship. When our marriages get into trouble, our entire society gets into trouble.

The signs that marriage is no longer a sacrament are all around us. Divorce, of course, is running rampant, with far too many of our modern marriages breaking up. We've come to accept divorce as a quick-and-sure cure for a difficult relationship. Yet divorce, while it can be soothing for a time, is not a cure for anything.

Any human relationship, including marriage, is going to involve some problems and perhaps some very hard times. But working through those hard times, finding solutions when there seem to be nothing but dead ends or impossible obstacles, will always result in stronger character in each spouse, as well as a stronger marriage relationship.

These days, though, we're much too impatient. Even in our churches, we'd rather resort to quick, easy answers rather than take our time and find the best solutions possible. The church has always been compassionate in dealing with problems in marriage. But in the past, many church leaders encouraged married couples to develop endurance and try to settle their differences before they fell back on divorce. The church was patient, in that it required seven years of separation for a husband and wife who were experiencing a rocky time in their relationship. Only after that seventh year could they be given a divorce.

My own parents went through this problem and actually decided on a temporary separation. But then they were reunited and, afterward, they developed a strong marriage—a truly *sacramental* union. Fortunately, my siblings and I were born after this reunion. So as you can see, I have a very personal interest in promoting enduring marital ties!

Of course, even when husbands and wives stay married, they may encounter plenty of problems. For one thing, if they lack a sense of the sacramental quality of marriage, they may feel free to be unfaithful to one another. This loose living of married people can completely undercut any marriage and rob a couple of the power to become "living stones" in building God's kingdom.

Sex, in a purely physical sense, has too often become the centerpiece of our marriages. So when sexual interest fades, the marriage itself may fall apart. We've become so hedonistic that we've come to expect that marriage is primarily supposed to make us "feel good." But this hedonism, which has in many cases supplanted a deeper, spirit-based relationship, will always betray us in the end.

As we know from various statistics from sociologists and other researchers, more than half of all married men and about half of all married women have been involved in at least one extramarital affair. It's no wonder that so many marriages are breaking up! The trust and the commitment that are so necessary to a permanent relationship have been lost as marriage has turned into a living together for the sake of convenience, rather than the sacrament that God meant it to be.

Husbands and wives may suffer from the terrible trend toward broken homes, but it's the children who suffer most. On the one hand, we claim that we love our children passionately. We want to give them the best that we possibly can, the advantages that prior generations didn't possess. But even as we give lip service to such values, we abort millions of children when the timing of their births doesn't quite suit us. We throw them out, like so many dirty rugs, rather than treat them as the spiritual creatures they really are.

Furthermore, many of those children who are finally born are born out of wedlock. Even celebrities in our culture, who are admired and followed by so many young people and adults alike, don't hesitate to have children before they get married. For that matter, many have children without ever getting married!

I realize, of course, that it may seem quite old-fashioned to be protesting such trends. But think about it for a moment:

Only twenty or thirty years ago, such practices would have been shocking and scandalous—in fact, in some cases, *criminal.* But today we have become desensitized. We have lost our sense of the spiritual dimension of marriage and also of the family. We proceed with our abortions, our illegitimate children, our premarital relationships, and various other practices with few if any feelings of guilt. Everyone else does it, so why shouldn't we? The old values and standards no longer apply—or so we're told.

But in fact, they *do* apply, and we are the losers when we fail to recognize God's will for us in our relationships. We think we are free to transgress the biblical standards, the moral and ethical principles that have been upheld for centuries in the traditions of the church. Yet what we are experiencing in our families and our society as a whole suggests otherwise.

Human relations are in worse shape today than perhaps ever before. Certainly, households are more divided. Increasingly, children live with only one parent. As a result, they lack the complete guidance and sense of familial wholeness that is necessary to their emotional and spiritual health.

In general, our society seems to have become increasingly self-centered. And at least part of the reason for this trend appears to be our lack of a commitment to the welfare of others. We're willing to end marriage relationships on the slightest pretext, rather than sacrifice our own interests to preserve and uphold the interests of others. Children and spouses are no longer as important as the interests of the individual who is trying to "realize his personal potential." As a people, we are all the losers for this pervasive selfishness.

But this is not the way God meant for things to be. The true purpose of marriage is not primarily pragmatic or utilitarian. Rather, marriage is the second most important divinely ordained relationship, after the person's relationship with God. When a Christian husband is united with a Christian wife, together they become united with God. I was impressed earlier in my ministry when I heard the late Bishop Fulton J. Sheen tell one of his audiences that the family knot should be comprised of three strands: the husband, the wife, and God. If you take God out, the relationship loses its meaning.

Jesus revealed another dimension of this marvelous mystery when he changed the water into wine at the marriage in Cana. Although the couple who were being married started off the wedding ceremony with some wine, there was not enough to get them through all the matrimonial festivities. But they were fortunate to have Jesus present with them!

First, he ordered that six stone jars be filled with water. Then, he turned the water into wine—wine that was not only abundant but that also was of a higher quality than the drink they had begun with.

The steward of the feast was so impressed that he told the bridegroom, "Every man serves the good wine first; and when men have drunk freely, then the poor wine; but you have kept the good wine until now." (John 2:10, RSV)

This first miracle of Jesus serves as a model for the entire marriage relationship. If Christ is present, binding the husband and wife together, their later years will be even sweeter and more satisfying than the early ones. And when God is the foundation, marriage becomes a holy sacrament, not just a convenient form of living together.

Finally, with God permeating every part of the relationship, the position of the children will be secure. A good marriage begins with a husband, a wife, and God, but it's completed with the arrival of children. I always admire young couples who plan their marriages so that they have some time to get to know each other before the children come along. At the same time, I think it's a big mistake to downplay or eliminate the role of the child in the family.

I've heard most of the objections: "Life is too expensive these days . . . education is too costly . . . children can tie you down." But I also realize something much more important: Nothing can be compared with the human child. I think that the child is the person Jesus had in mind when he said, "For what is a man profited if he shall gain the whole world, and lose his own soul?" (Matthew 16:26, KJV)

The child is the very soul of our society. Parents may think that they can achieve the greatest enjoyment by going out to a party on Saturday night or otherwise entertaining themselves. But in fact, the greatest joy for parents is the child. I have not yet seen—and I hope that I will never see—a Christian couple who were not happy with their child.

When the child becomes an integral part of the husband-wife-God family bond, a network of relationships is established that is likely to continue for a lifetime. The children learn from godly parents what it means to give to others and sacrifice one's own interests for them. Thus, the groundwork is laid for future generations to continue those traditions that began with the sacramental marriage.

I'm reminded here of my two sisters, who were brought up by our devout parents on the Aegean island of Imbros. As a result of this Christian background, they each developed a strong faith and a sense of the importance of sacrifice for others.

In fact, I was the one who benefited the most from their sacrifice, as they stayed at home and worked hard to provide additional money so that I could be able to continue my theological studies. Without their help, it would have been much more difficult, if not impossible, for me to reach my present position. And I must say, their example, as well as that of my parents, has made me much more aware of how important it is to return in some small way to others what I have been so fortunate to receive.

Yet despite my deep commitment to the principles of Christian marriage, I myself have chosen to remain unmarried —to be celibate in the tradition of St. Paul and others who have relinquished their right to raise a family because of the demands of ministry. Certainly, I don't think my unmarried condition makes me any better than any other Christian; my calling is just different from those who have chosen to take a wife.

THE HARD PATH OF CELIBACY

If God had wanted most people to remain unmarried, I think Jesus would have told us this during his ministry here on earth. But he didn't. Even St. Paul, who said that he wished all were unmarried as he was, acknowledged that celibacy is a special gift, and certainly a gift that is *not* given to most people.

If a husband and wife can get their priorities in order, so that God's work comes first with them, they can certainly serve God through their family at least as well—and perhaps they can serve him even better—than can a person who is not married.

But still, some people *are* called to serve God in an unmarried state. And their choice and gift should be honored by those in other positions in the church. If a person feels called to a monastic life, he may be able to pray and study more extensively and intensely, for hour upon hour each day, if he has only himself to worry about. Also, in our church as well as in some others, there are other quite valid traditions of celibacy among members of the clergy.

On the other hand, celibacy is an extremely serious business. I've occasionally encountered some clergy who have said, "I'm single, but I'm not celibate." Or, "I'm celibate, but I'm not chaste."

By this, they mean that even though they are not married, they still feel free to have all sorts of sexual relationships, with no regrets or remorse. That attitude is a complete travesty, not to mention a total misunderstanding of what celibacy is all about. Since the third or fourth century, the church has recognized that the burden of celibacy is something that shouldn't be placed on a person who is unable to bear it. If you choose to be celibate, then that means you will not only refrain from getting married; you will also refrain from all sexual liaisons. You will remain pure, as Jesus said the unmarried should remain pure.

There's an old canon that goes back to the fourth century, at the First Ecumenical Council, requiring that a personal choice of celibacy couldn't be made final until a person was twenty-five years of age. Today, however, this canon isn't always applied strictly.

In my own case, I was ordained when I was just twenty-three years of age, and I took my vows of celibacy at that time. But despite my own experience, I believe that the ancient canon should be enforced today. Why? For one thing, it's important for a person to grow a little older, past the first sexual flush of youth, before he takes a final vow never to be married. Also, to reach the office of bishop in the hierarchy of our church a person must be celibate, and that can encourage a link between celibacy and ambition in the church. As far as

I'm concerned, those who at an early age feel they want to be bishops, should be brought to their knees in prayer before they make the choice to be celibate. Ambition is never a good reason to stay unmarried, and if ambition is a person's *only* motivation, the vow he has taken will most likely be broken.

I have told younger members of the clergy, "If you violate your vows, the punishment you receive won't just be one that will be meted out by the church. The greatest punishment of all will come from your own conscience."

To sum up, then, celibacy is a condition that is appropriate only for a small number of men or women who feel called to dedicate all their time and energy to the work of God, and especially to prayer.

For most people, however, marriage, in its sacramental, God-infused form, should be the norm. From time immemorial, God has worked through the union of husbands and wives to produce godly children, who in turn will carry on the traditions of the faith in lifetimes to come. In most cases, this marriage relationship is the highest calling a person can hear from God, the most powerful means available to follow on this earth the footsteps of Jesus.

22

Christ in Art

Since the time of Christ, artists have tried to capture the essence of Christian spirituality in their paintings, sculptures and other creations. For that matter, even in Old Testament times, God anointed certain artisans and craftsmen, such as Bezalel, who built the ancient Hebrew tabernacle and the Ark of the Covenant.

"I have filled him with the Spirit of God," God said of Bezalel, "with ability and intelligence, with knowledge and all craftsmanship, to devise artistic designs to work in gold, silver, and bronze, in cutting stones for setting, and in carving wood, for work in every craft." (Exodus 31:3–5, RSV)

Still, despite these traditions of religious art and craftsmanship, controversies have often arisen about the use of art in worship. Some opponents of religious art would invoke the second of the Ten Commandments, prohibiting the use of "graven images" or "any likeness of anything that is in heaven

above, or that is in the earth beneath, or that is in the water
under the earth." This command, they would say, effectively
eliminates the possibility of using artwork in our churches.
Also, various politically inspired opposition movements, such
as those involving the so-called "iconoclasts" in the eighth and
ninth centuries A.D., have called the use of church art into
question.

But for me, the use of the icon—from the Greek *eikon,* or
"image"—can be quite inspiring. In any case, the icon certainly represents no threat to genuine biblical tradition.

Generally speaking, the icons we use in Orthodox
Churches are two-dimensional representations of Christ, his
mother Mary, or one of the saints. Sometimes, they may be
made of ivory or some ceramic material; other times, they may
be wooden images, painted with oils.

In the words of one of the saints, icons are "the open
books," which God can use to talk directly to us. They're not
simply decorations, but rather are channels of God's blessing
that he can use to guide us and respond to our needs.

I myself certainly accept the icons as more than mere
statues. In a way, they sometimes seem like human beings. I
can touch them and feel a deep sense of reverence and admira-
tion for the person whom they depict. Many people I know
will proudly show others photographs of their children passionately kissing an icon. For that matter, I love to kiss them
myself, especially those of Christ or of one of the saints like St.
Basil the Great, whom I've always admired.

But when I do this, am I worshiping the icon itself, the
physical representation? By no means! As I've said, they are
the open books through which God communicates to me.
When I kneel before the icon, or kiss it, I know that the reverence I feel is going directly to God himself. And God may also

deal with me directly, either to communicate some special word, or even to perform a miracle such as healing.

These days, it may be difficult for those brought up on television and the startling special effects in our movies to understand how significant icons have been to Christian believers over the centuries. But remember: For hundreds of years, most people couldn't read. And even if they could, they might not have had easy access to the Bible. As a result, statues and paintings became extremely important in communicating the Gospel message, especially beginning in the fifth through seventh centuries A.D. By learning about the great church leaders and martyrs through art, those who were unable to read could understand better how to live out their faith, day by day.

Also, you're well aware that we use various audio-visual techniques today, such as cassette tapes, videotapes, slides, and moving pictures, for religious communications. Similarly, the ancient communicators of the Gospel relied on icons, as well as the liturgical readings and processions, to get their message across. In addition, many people just don't enjoy reading and studying books. They'd rather get their information through the visual and auditory media, and that's much the way many other Christians have felt through the centuries.

Of course, some artworks are more effective at communicating the message of Christ than others. I'm not particularly moved by the paintings of some Byzantine artisans, who presented Jesus as the "Pantocrator." As I look into some of those dark Byzantine eyes, with brows so heavy that they join together, I feel that the look of those Christs is cutting right through me—but it's not the look of a person who is able to love.

On the other hand, when I stand before the much later works of El Greco, who in some ways was an heir of the

Byzantine tradition, I see a Jesus with more humanity and tenderness. Even those long, almost emaciated figures of the Savior have a face that I can respond to as a true person, a Master who is deeply concerned with me and my welfare.

Christian art, then, including the icons, is simply another way of communicating in concrete terms the love of God to men and women. Some people—especially those who are visually oriented—may leave a museum or a church with a new and lasting impression of Christ, his mother Mary, or some saint. And the message they get may be one they never could have received from mere reading.

The humanity of Christ and of his followers throughout the ages is an essential part of our spiritual understanding and development. We must not only acknowledge with our minds that Jesus was fully human, but we must also *feel* his humanity, deep within our souls. Sometimes, then, to achieve the deepest experience of the incarnation, it's necessary to engage the eyes, the ears, and the touch, as well as the rational faculties of our minds. At such moments, it may be helpful to focus on an image, an *eikon,* that can serve as God's special channel of blessing.

23

Is There Hope for Political Activism?

During the mid-1960s, I became deeply committed to the cause of civil rights. As a result, I got involved in the marches and protests that condemned segregation and pushed for protective rights legislation.

During this period, some people regarded me as a mindless liberal. Others, including some members of my own church, labeled me a traitor because they believed I had betrayed the people of the South.

But I went ahead with the marches and with the political activism because I believed then—and I still believe—that a Christian must do what his conscience tells him to do. If I feel God moving me in a certain direction and I fail to respond, I become a "clanging cymbal," as St. Paul puts it in his First Epistle to the Corinthians.

Today, after several decades of being involved in activist causes and dealing extensively with social and political leaders,

I still believe in fighting for justice and equality among all peoples. I also believe in promoting peace, both on the domestic scene and in broader global arenas, where nations rattle their sabers, display their missiles, and threaten mutual annihilation.

But at the same time, I think I've become somewhat more realistic about the possibilities for activism, both now and in the future. I know that in all forms of activism, I must, as Jesus said, do the will of the Father. And what is the will of the Father? St. Paul defines it very clearly in 1 Timothy 2:4, where he says that God "will have all men to be saved, and to come unto the knowledge of the truth." (KJV)

God, in other words, has a deeply *personal* concern for each one of us. It's his will that you and I and every other individual man and woman on earth should know him and be saved by him. As a result, all of our activism should be directed toward the ultimate end of bringing individuals into contact with the saving power of Christ.

So when I'm presented with an opportunity to be an activist, I often ask myself a series of questions, which help me focus on whether the planned action will be a channel for the realization of God's will in this world. I'll ask:

What inspires this activism?

Is it an abstract philosophy, or real compassion for men and women?

What motives lie behind the demonstrations that are planned?

When we plan our parades, will we parade as we do on Easter, to proclaim the Resurrection?

Will we parade so that social justice will prevail, or so that individual, selfish interests of the demonstrators can be served?

Will we parade so that human dignity may be restored, or so that the leaders and organizers of the demonstration can feed their egos?

Will we parade enthusiastically, even if no one notices us? Or will we only be satisfied if—God forbid—we get stories in the newspapers and on TV so that everyone will notice us?

The more public and open we get with our political activism, the greater the danger that our motives will be marred by our own self-interest. To combat this tendency, I've formulated what I call the "Seven Commandments for Christian Activism." This is certainly not an exhaustive list. But I hope that these points will help you, as they've helped me, think and reflect more fully on what my real purposes and motives are as I join with others in social and political movements.

Commandment #1: Avoid headlines.

This commandment speaks for itself. I believe that one of the greatest dangers in any activist movement is that the leaders will become tempted by the fame and notoriety associated with extensive press coverage. If this happens, too often they lose sight of their original goals.

Seeing your name and picture plastered across newspaper headlines can be a heady experience, and seeing your image projected on television newscasts to thousands or even millions of viewers can definitely inflate the ego. But such fame, notoriety, and high-profile coverage runs contrary to most of what Jesus did during his lifetime.

As you'll recall, Christ avoided publicity as much as possible, especially during the early years of his ministry. As much as possible, he did his work on the grassroots level, out of the glare of public notice. It was only later, after his ministry had been solidly established and his disciples reasonably well versed in the ways of their Master—that broader recognition came to him. And even at the end of his life, relatively few people knew who he was or what he had done—at least few in comparison with many of our "media stars" today.

Commandment #2: Forget liberal-conservative distinctions.

As far as I'm concerned, liberalism and conservatism are two of the most detrimental inventions of the modern mind. Once you get branded as a liberal, conservatives won't listen to you. Conversely, if you're known as a conservative, you probably won't have any audience with liberals.

Remember: Our ultimate objective as Christian activists is to show compassion to individual human beings on as broad a scale as possible. That means avoiding political labels and focusing not on the philosophy or the cause, but rather on the individual man or woman in need.

Jesus' opponents tried to label him so that they could put him in a political or theological pigeonhole and thus deal with him more easily. So, when he reinterpreted some of the teachings of the Old Testament, such as the observance of the Sabbath, the Pharisees accused him of subverting important Jewish traditions.

But Jesus often responded by pointing to the needs of specific individuals. He healed on the Sabbath because individuals needed healing, not because he was overly concerned with theological niceties. Jesus' main aim and struggle was to liberate people from the letter of the law and open their eyes to the Spirit. He knew that, in so doing, he would also open their hearts to show greater love and compassion for their fellow human beings.

Commandment #3: Be suspicious of trendy issues.

Sometimes, as with the civil rights movement, the underlying purpose of political activism may be clearly in harmony with God's will. But other times, the issues which give rise to activism are much more questionable and may even be contrary to what God wants in our society and our relationships.

Some people, for example, have a particular image of a "Christian America," which they picture as a return to some comfortable life of the past, a life which probably never existed. Such a nostalgic vision of our society often includes erroneous, homogeneous, and sectarian views of what we as Americans and Christians are all about.

On the other hand, other movements may arise not out of narrow-minded nostalgia, but out of the pervasive bankruptcy of morals from which we suffer. Recently, I watched a television show where two homosexual men and one lesbian told about how they plan to adopt a child. Certainly, I'm not in favor of persecuting homosexuals. But at the same time, I know that homosexuality is not part of the natural order of things. Those relationships are not part of God's will or plan for human beings. Therefore, I could never see how an authentic Christian activist could get involved in a pro-homosexual movement or promote causes such as the adoption of children by homosexuals. Christ came to liberate us from our old, sinful way of life and to introduce us to a new freedom under God. But legalization of the illegal is not liberation from anything.

Similarly, many politicians and social activists have gotten involved in promoting abortion in the name of women's rights or freedom of sexual expression. As a matter of fact, in recent years, the United States has spent billions of dollars financing and subsidizing abortion centers.

Such expenditures show that we're indeed a crazy society, with crazy standards! Our moral values have, in many cases, gone completely haywire. But the activists in such areas are often content to say, "Abortion is not a moral issue—it's just a practical choice that people in our society have a right to make."

To get involved in such a corrupt, trendy way of thinking is tantamount to abdicating any moral responsibility that attaches to troublesome issues and concerns.

Commandment #4: Take time to think.

In most cases, we could avoid the trap of trendy issues if we would just stop and spend some time in serious thought and prayer. Too often these days, we react without thinking at all. Many times, we'll automatically support a certain movement, such as by signing a petition or giving some money, just because a friend asked us to. We don't take time to think about the implications of our actions.

Or even if we do think a little, we may respond in a certain way just to convince another person or another group that we're really concerned and informed people. We may want to be regarded as "enlightened" or "liberal" or "conservative" depending upon the peer group we've identified with. So, without asking God what *he* thinks, we join the crowd and support the cause that's presented to us.

This attitude reminds me of Paul's description of himself in 1 Corinthians 13: "When I was a child, I spoke like a child, I thought like a child, I reasoned like a child; when I became a man, I gave up childish ways." (RSV)

We, too, must give up our childish, unthinking, non-praying approach to life and spend a few minutes, hours, or even days with God before we decide to commit ourselves to an activist cause. Talking and reasoning with God in prayer and discussing a prospective course of action with other believers will clarify any issue you confront. Also, as you seek God's will, you can expect him to give you a sense of assurance when you find the right path. Taking some time to think and pray is the best way to put yourself in touch with God and the path of activism he may have chosen for you.

Commandment #5: In most cases, focus on immediate issues, rather than on those that are far away.

Usually, God wants us first to get deeply involved in our local neighborhoods, towns, and cities. Being of Greek origin, I come from a small, close-knit society. Also, being a member of a minority religion in today's world, I have a sense of the insular quality of many neighborhoods and communities, with their very special concerns and problems. For these and other reasons, I'm particularly sensitive to the importance of dealing with the problems and needs of those with whom we are in immediate contact, rather than concentrating on those who are far away.

Of course, we should be aware of what's going on in far-flung places and nations, and whenever possible, we should make our voices heard in the causes of truth and justice. But more often than not, the average person can do little to affect the cosmic course of events. To be sure, you can vote; you can sign petitions; you can give money to important causes; and you can even get out on the streets and demonstrate when an issue seems particularly important and pressing. But a life that is devoted only to broad, global issues tends to be a life that lacks the impact that can be exerted by those who focus on the near-at-hand.

In short, I think that most of us should pay attention

primarily to what's happening in the streets, politics, and social systems of the city or town where we live, rather than on events in Central America, the Middle East, or other distant places. Instead of spending all of our time worrying and talking about a war thousands of miles away—and that's often all we *can* do, just worry and talk—we should be teaching our children how to develop strong values. We should be cleaning up the local environment. We should be caring for the sick and oppressed within arms' reach. Then, if these immediate issues lead naturally to involvement in a more distant concern, we'll be in a much stronger position to take effective action and exercise more powerful leadership.

One young woman, for example, became deeply concerned about the plight of Vietnamese and Cambodian refugees who fled to the United States after the fall of Saigon in 1975. As a result, she established a refugee committee in her church. Then, with the help of several dozen fellow believers, she was able to help more than twenty refugees make the transition from their own war-torn countries to the United States.

Clearly, this young woman was involved in an issue that concerned her local community: Her local church was the primary instrument through which the refugees were settled. Also, all of the refugees moved into homes or apartments in the neighborhood.

Then, after engaging in this local, grassroots activism for a couple of years, this young woman became aware of a broader, political problem facing the refugees: She learned of the plight of the "boat people," who were trying to leave Vietnam on small boats and makeshift rafts, but were running into serious problems, including pirates on the South China Sea. She came to feel that the U.S. Government was doing too little to help these boat people. So she started a letter-writing and petitioning campaign designed both to influence congressmen and senators to pass legislation and to put pressure on the White House to help the boat people.

This young woman could have begun such a campaign without her background as a person who had worked extensively with individual refugees. But her prior willingness to devote her time to individuals in need gave her tremendous credibility and important contacts, which made her political efforts much more effective. Also, the political activism arose *naturally* from more immediate concerns in her community.

As we've seen before, it's important for all of our activities in this world to begin with the care and concern for the individual human soul. Jesus didn't promote a movement of mass ethics or morals. Rather, he centered on the conversion, spiritual growth and good health of the individual.

Sometimes, I think that those who live their lives focusing on faraway issues are afraid to confront themselves and the problems of their immediate surroundings. Also, they may be hesitant to look deep within their own souls to examine their own relationship with God.

God is always nearby, ready to respond when we make ourselves available to him. But too many people—including many activists who like to rail against the wars and rumors of war, the famines and injustices on distant shores—have placed God, like the political and social issues, in a faraway place. If he exists at all for these people, he's limited to some distant spot in a heaven that is completely separated from the real world.

But that's not the God of Abraham, Isaac, and Jacob. That's not the God who came to earth and died on the cross for each of us as individuals. The *real* God is not far away at all. He's right here, in our midst. And if we'll only let him, he can also enter our hearts and transform us into truly effective and caring activists.

Commandment #6: Follow your Christian conscience.

So far, many of the "commandments" that we've been discussing are rooted in good analysis and logic. But it's not always possible to make decisions based on pure reason. Instead, you must open yourself up and allow God to break through into your deepest being. That may mean evading or even shattering some of the barriers that we raise in the logical parts of our minds.

Jesus told Nicodemus that the Spirit of God is like the wind, blowing here and there as it wills. And that's precisely the way the Spirit moves among us today. Sometimes, as we pray and wait and listen for God's guidance, it may be necessary to accept a strong mental impression followed by a sense of certainty. Then, we act on that certainty, even if it's not possible to analyze it completely or reason out every detail. God uses our conscience, our innate sense of right and wrong, to give us these spiritual impressions and also to provide the sense of certainty that those impressions can bring.

So I would say feel free, once you've used your logical faculties to their limit, to rely on your conscience. Look to "holy intuition" when you make decisions about activist projects. And, finally, you'll find that you can act with even greater assurance if you allow your conscience always to be guided and tested by the Scripture—a fact that brings us to our final commandment.

Commandment #7: To illuminate your conscience, look to the Bible.

As Christians, we emphasize the importance of the individual's relationship with God and of personal spiritual development. At the same time, however, our faith is not atomistic, with individuals existing separately, operating completely independently of one another in some sort of vacuum. Rather the Christian faith requires a community of individuals, relating intimately to one another, even as they relate individually and corporately to God.

Furthermore, as we enter into this network of relationships, we have access to constant guidance and correction in our decisions and actions from a number of outside sources. These include the encouragement and advice of other believers, the answers that God provides for our prayers, and the standards and guidance contained in Scripture.

The regular reading and study of the Bible is an absolutely essential element in keeping our consciences true and God-centered in all the challenges of life. With the Bible illuminating our consciences, we find we are in a better position to know the will of God when we're confronted with decisions about becoming political or social activists.

Clearly, if an issue that you are considering conflicts with the clear moral teachings of Scripture, you should drop that issue and move on to something else. If the issue seems questionable in light of Scripture, then perhaps you'll need to spend extra time in prayer or consultation with other believers whom you trust. But in any event, the Bible is always an important starting place for making such decisions, and many times, the written Word may be completely sufficient in itself.

Now that I'm in my mid-seventies and have been through many "wars" in the social and political arenas, I'm more hesitant to dive headlong into every seemingly valid issue that comes to my attention. It's easy, in the excitement and energy of youth, to plunge into causes without really thinking them through and weighing their importance in light of the time and energy that are available.

When you're young, it sometimes seems that there's time to do anything you like—and certainly there *is* more time than when you get older. But don't assume, if you're relatively young, that you can get involved in any issue that comes along with no repercussions for your spiritual growth or the growth of others. If you begin to promote a cause that conflicts with the fundamental tenets of the faith, you may feel the consequences for years afterward, and sometimes for your entire life. Also, if you get sidetracked into meaningless or marginal activist activities, you'll soon find, no matter how young you are, that there are better things to do with your time and better ways to promote the welfare of others.

The footsteps of Jesus are activist footsteps, in that they don't just stand in one spot. They keep moving ahead, steadily surmounting every obstacle and challenge in their path. But these footsteps have a direction. They are not just leading you in circles or in a way that seems for the moment to be worthy and helpful, but later turns out to be a wrong turn. Rather, they are leading you, step by step, to Jesus himself, and he is the one toward whom all your activist efforts should be directed.

24

Servanthood:
The End, Not the Means

Jesus confronted his disciples with many difficult sayings. But perhaps the most difficult for many of them was this: ". . . whoever would be great among you must be your servant, and whoever would be first among you must be your slave."*

The teachings of the Savior include many such paradoxical statements, and it would take more than a lifetime for us to understand every implication of what he was really saying. His teachings on servanthood are among the most difficult to comprehend because, as much as anything he said, they go against the grain of normal human experience and understanding.

After all, by contemporary standards, if you want to be "great," then it's necessary to excel, achieve, and rise up step by step in your particular profession or business. The final goal is to become the best, so that you stand head and shoulders

* Matthew 20:26–27, RSV.

above everyone else. Such prestige and status almost always carries with it the possibility of power, of "lording it over" others who haven't advanced quite as far as you have.

But Jesus quickly recognized this drift in human thought, and just as quickly he dismissed it: He told his disciples that the rulers of the gentiles "lorded it over" those who were beneath them, but the followers of Christ were not to use that approach as the standard. They were to be more humble; they were to count themselves as less than others; instead of behaving as the eldest, they were to behave as the youngest.

In short, those who follow Jesus must serve, rather than be served. They must wash the feet of others, rather than have their own feet washed. They must bear the burdens of others, rather than expect others to shoulder their concerns and cares.

But even as I say these words, I know that it's very difficult to communicate what they really mean. Too often, Christians think they understand what it means to be a servant. Then, they go out and give of themselves for a time, and they may actually do some good and help some other people in the process.

But still, too often, these seeming servants tend to see service as a means to an end, rather than an end in itself. With Jesus, though, being a servant isn't a stage one goes through in an upward movement toward spiritual perfection. Rather, true Christian spiritual growth almost seems to be a *downward* trek, as we travel from one act of service to another and another, each of which may involve increasingly greater humility and self-sacrifice.

The life of Jesus himself can be a sobering model for those who, like James and John, hope to advance by "putting in their time" for awhile in this life. Then, they expect to move up, step by step to greater glory, notoriety, and authority in the Kingdom of God. To be sure, there are rewards that await those who have used their gifts well and who have diligently sought the will of God. But the prospect of such rewards, whatever they may be, must not become our major motive for service.

Rather, what we should expect is increasingly greater challenges, which will allow us to become even more humble servants year by year. We should anticipate having our egos, our very *selves,* decrease, as John the Baptist said, at the same time that Jesus himself increases. So servanthood must be the ultimate end toward which we aspire, and not the means to achieve some ultimate state of glory, which may be just a figment of our human fantasies.

Yet an important part of the paradox in all this is that, while such radical servanthood might seem to be depressing and unattractive from a human point of view, from God's point of view—and ultimately from our own—it's an experience of great beauty and excitement. Only by becoming a servant can we really experience love, joy, peace, and those other inner fruits that can give life supreme exuberance, satisfaction, and meaning. By seeking to love, help, and serve others, as Jesus did, we give fully of our inner resources. In fact, at times it may seem that we've completely emptied ourselves. But at the same time, by such serving, we will open ourselves to receive blessings from God that transcend our wildest dreams.

In a way, Jesus' words in the fourteenth chapter of St. John's Gospel sum up for me both the demands and potential of the true servant of Christ. There, he says that those who believe in him and follow him will do the works he did, and even greater works. All that's necessary is to remain committed to him, to follow in his footsteps, and to ask our desires in his name.

But even as we ask, we must be obedient. We must keep his commandments and follow the guidance of the Spirit of Truth, whom he promised would dwell with us and in us. And as we obey and follow, we will gain access to his power and experience his peace.

Clearly, the servanthood of Jesus is similar to human servanthood only in certain superficial ways. To be sure, we must do work for others, help them, love them, and even submit ourselves to them. But even as we serve them, we also serve Christ himself. And the more we serve, the more we feel the glow of his presence and enjoy the potential of his power.

Of course, this kind of servanthood is never something we can attain completely in this life. It's something that is always just out of reach, just beyond our human grasp. But even at my age, nothing attracts me so much as the unapproachable and the unclimbable, the spiritual blessing that I experience in part but still don't have firmly in my grasp. I can only say that what I have tasted and experienced so far of the life of faith in Christ makes me want more and more. And day by day, my faith is transformed, as the Epistle to the Hebrews says, with a greater assurance that those things I now hope for will one day be a complete reality in my life.